Praise for *The Secret Despair of the Secular Left*

"*The Secret Despair of the Secular Left* is a *cri de coeur* that makes us sit up in our chairs and reconsider our lives. In this engaging, not easily pigeonholed book, Levy-Lyons details how secular liberal values have resulted in devastating disconnection from our deepest selves, our communities and our planet. Drawing from Judaism and other religious traditions, philosophers and social justice thinkers, as well as her own experience as a spiritual leader, she challenges us to recommit to responsibility, embodied connection and awe."
— **Rabbi Lisa Goldstein**, teacher, spiritual director, and former leader of the Institute for Jewish Spirituality

"*The Secret Despair of the Secular Left* is an insightful, moving, and wise meditation on our contemporary condition. But this is no abstract analysis! With honesty, grace, and soulfulness, Ana Levy-Lyons shares her own psycho-spiritual journey and remarkable stories she has gathered along the way to help us understand the sources of the diseases of despair and loneliness afflicting our society: disconnection from each other, dislocation from our earth, and disembodiment from our selves. Read this book and you will not only find illumination and inspiration but an authentic path for human flourishing."
— **Irwin Kula**, president emeritus of Clal: The National Jewish Center for Learning and Leadership

"Ana Levy-Lyons gives voice to grief, grief that realizes we've been duped. It's not fame and followers we need or want. It's not the perfect pair of jeans on the perfectly sculpted backside. What we are hungry for is authentic community, grounded in cultural traditions, connected to our precious bodies, living on this sacred and generous planet. We want to be part of something greater than ourselves. Levy-Lyons helps show us the way back."

— **Rev. Adriene Thorne,** senior minister, The Riverside Church in the City of New York

"*The Secret Despair of the Secular Left* is a powerful and intimate journey into the heart of our disenchanted world. It will be an eye-opening read for anyone with a nagging sense that something is wrong in our post-religious, tech-happy era, but can't quite put a finger on it. Levy-Lyons lifts up the stories of ordinary people and interprets them as if they were dreams, allowing us to climb inside them, look around, and understand our lives at a deeper level. She gently invites us to see the layers of grief and loss just below the surface. In naming the hidden losses of our modern era, this book gives voice to our deepest yearnings for real connection. It can empower us and inspire us to move toward change."

— **Rabbi David A. Ingber,** founding rabbi of Romemu, and Senior Director for Jewish Life and the Bronfman Center at 92NY

The Secret Despair
of the Secular Left

Also by Ana Levy-Lyons

No Other Gods: The Politics of the Ten Commandments

THE SECRET DESPAIR OF THE SECULAR LEFT

Our Fraying Connections *with* Our Communities, Our Bodies, *and the* Earth

ANA LEVY-LYONS

BROADLEAF BOOKS
MINNEAPOLIS

THE SECRET DESPAIR OF THE SECULAR LEFT
Our Fraying Connections with Our Communities, Our Bodies, and the Earth

Copyright © 2025 Ana Levy-Lyons. Published by Broadleaf Books. All rights reserved. Except for brief quotations in critical articles or reviews, no part of this book may be reproduced in any manner without prior written permission from the publisher. Email copyright@broadleafbooks.com or write to Permissions, Broadleaf Books, PO Box 1209, Minneapolis, MN 55440-1209.

29 28 27 26 25 24   1 2 3 4 5 6 7 8 9

Library of Congress Control Number: 2024946053 (print)

Cover illustration by Kristi Smith
Cover design by Jay Smith—Juicebox Designs

Print ISBN: 978-1-5064-8625-3
eBook ISBN: 978-1-5064-8626-0

Printed in India.

For Miriam and Micah,
with a prayer
that all of your days will be
days of awe

Contents

Unrealized Loss	1
Surplus Grief in Modern Death	23
The Secular Gaze	33
Where Did All the Religious Flower Children Go?	51
Loss of Intimacy	61
Covering the Mirrors	69
Contactless	77
Living in a Material World	95
Pe'ah—The Wild, Holy Edge	107
It's the Thought That Counts	127
Spiritual Bypass and the Caging of the Yetzer Ha-Ra	133
Breasts	145
Being Worthwhile	159
Bicycle-Powered Light Bulbs and Sand Mandalas	175
Worrying Just the Right Amount	187
Days of Awe	199
Acknowledgments	211
Notes	215

Unrealized Loss

During the early weeks of the coronavirus pandemic, the stock market plunged. Some people sold their holdings in a panic, and some were forced to sell because they needed the money. Others held on in hopes that this was just a financial bad dream from which we would all awaken. They held their breath through that liminal moment, waiting to see if their investments would really turn out to be worth only a fraction of what they had paid. Economists have a term for the loss incurred when an asset has decreased in value but hasn't yet been sold: it is an "unrealized loss." It's only when the investor sells the stock that the loss becomes real and the money is gone.

This book explores a different kind of unrealized loss—not of money but of sacred relationships with one another, with the earth, and with our own bodies. I call these sacred relationships because in my experience it is through these relationships that we encounter God. And the fraying of these relationships has happened concurrently with the fading of religious life since the mid-twentieth century, especially among more metropolitan, left-leaning denizens of Western nations.

In the modern era, our society has made a panoply of institutional, cultural, and ideological investments. We have invested in technology, global mobility, science, convenience, pleasure, and an ethic of rights-based individualism and personal actualization. On the surface, these investments have paid great dividends. They have made people's lives better in measurable ways. But they have been expensive. They have come at the cost of other investments we could make—in religious life, local community, ethnic and cultural traditions, serious spiritual practice, and increasingly our capacity for being physically present with others in meaningful conversation and connection. The opportunity cost for these investments has been momentous. Most disastrously, we have failed to invest in the land and all the creatures with whom our fate is enmeshed.

Like an overvalued stock, our investments can cruise along happily until there is a crisis. But when we're forced to sell—when we have to use the resources into which we've sunk our life energy—then we learn their true value. This is the moment at which we find ourselves today. Our investments are failing us. The early twenty-first century is widely recognized as an era of social and ecological disintegration. Without rehearsing the entire litany of misery, suffice it to say that deaths of despair, depression, anxiety, economic inequality, and extreme political polarization are on the rise. We proved inept at acting collaboratively to fight a global pandemic. And we are witnessing the storms, droughts, and fires that signal the real-time unraveling of the ecosystems of our planet.

In our panic we look to our now-familiar saviors—the experts of science and economics and the sages of self-improvement. But despite the treasure trove of knowledge that they offer us, we find ourselves still foundering. When it comes to the big questions of life and death, God, meaning, purpose, or love, the experts run out of words. Science can tell us the efficacy of masks in preventing COVID-19 transmission, but it cannot say how the freedom of individuals should balance against the interests of public health. A TED Talk might tell us how to make ourselves 10 percent happier, but it cannot weigh the value of happiness itself as a goal. A website can list a hundred burial and cremation options, but it cannot hold us and teach us what to do with our own loved one's body when they die. These are matters of spirit and wisdom carried in communities of faith, cultural traditions, and divine revelation. And these are the investments that we find lacking when we really need them, like today, when we are in crisis and we are forced to sell.

Raised Nothing

I grew up in a secular household. We celebrated Christmas and Easter as American holidays, but my parents were atheists, my father stridently so. I was taught that religious people were a little like sheep, blindly following the leader, dimly believing the comforting myths about the "sky fairy." I did not want to be a sheep.

My parents were Jewish by heritage but so disconnected from the tradition that it never came up. That's the mild way to put it. Beneath that disconnection lay great pain—the antisemitism of 1940s New Jersey (where they each grew up), the sense of being stifled by religious and family obligations, and the belief that they were being deprived of a wider, more wondrous world. My parents needed to escape, and this meant shedding their class and ethnicity like a putrid skin. Each saw assimilation as their only way out of the embarrassing superstitions, oppressive rules, and tacky taste of their communities.

And so they never mentioned that they (and therefore I) were Jewish. They (and therefore I) had little contact with our extended family. Religion and heritage, like anything else, were merely options, and we had opted out. In my understanding, as a white, upper-middle-class, geographically mobile, vaguely culturally Christian family, we were simply "nothing"—devoid of any limiting particularities. This itself constituted the American dream for us. We were free to be exactly who we wanted to be at all times. In the words of the classic feminist album that was on loop in my childhood home, we were "free to be you and me." And, what's more, being nothing in this way conferred superiority over others who remained shackled to Old World ways.

This kind of self-assured nothingness does in fact confer immense privilege in our society. It casts the individual, male, "rational" agent as the norm from which others deviate (in ways that should be tolerated but never centered). From its omniscient perch, he can take cool, anthropological interest in the Baptist who actually believes in the virgin birth, the Orthodox Jew who dresses like it's nineteenth-century Poland, or the Kentucky farmer who's never left the county in which he was born. Most important, nothingness suggests unlimited freedom of body and mind. Because I am ontologically nothing in particular, I can be anything. I am not tethered to any one place, community, tradition, history, sex, or even my own physical limitations. Everything I see is malleable, and everything I do is every day a fresh choice.

I enjoyed this privilege for a time and would have fiercely defended it as the best way to live. Everyone should try it! But eventually I found that at the heart of this nothingness was a profound emptiness. I had financial privilege but spiritual poverty.

Along with the absence of religious ties in my upbringing came an absence of ties to anything or anyone else. My parents separated when I was young, and for the first eight years of my life I did not live in one place or even one country for more than a couple of years. I had no connection to a piece of land or a place with any ancestral history. Without strong extended family connections, there was no circle of adults and children in my life whom I would call "my community," no people whom I would call "my people." And my body was not a sacred vessel but a machine to be shaped toward the fulfillment of my ambitions.

I have come to believe that this is not just my story but the defining story of our time. It's the story of disembodiment, disconnection, and dislocation. It cuts across class and race. When it's told of poor and working-class children, the language is different—rather than "freedom," it's often framed in terms of "broken homes," addiction, and poverty. Rather than choosing to move for career opportunities, parents might be forced to move because of job losses or gentrification. Rather than libertine sexual mores, it might be economic stress that drives divorce. Rather than communities evaporating through upward mobility and brain drain, they might be destroyed by a new highway built through their neighborhood or by the local toxic waste site sickening pregnant women. And to be sure, an unstable and disconnected childhood is far more traumatic when the instability and disconnection are forced on the family.

But in some ways, mine is the privileged edition of the same book. For the elites and would-be elites, like my parents (who were striving to join the upper class with an earnest fake-it-till-you-make-it determination), it's framed as a story of choice and self-creation. It reflects a classic second-generation immigrant ethic: Now that material security has been hard-won by the previous generation, we can move up in Maslow's hierarchy of needs and seek self-actualization. The child who comes along for this ride is endowed with infinite possibilities, something the parents never had. It seems like the perfect gift.

For me and for many others of my generation, class, and culture, however, it's a gift that (unbeknownst to the well-meaning parents) comes bundled with a burglary. For these children, without God, without the proverbial village to raise them, without meaningful traditions to connect to the past and the future, without a piece of earth to call home, without a reverence for the miracle of their bodies, they have nothing that belongs to them. Nothing is a given; everything is contingent. Raised as "nothing," the children's worth is attested by nothing beyond themselves. They feel loved, not with an infinite divine love, but only in the earnest yet uneven ways that we humans are able to love each other. They have no purpose larger than what they want out of life. Success is defined by the culture. And meaning-making is entirely up to the individual.

I eventually found my way back to Judaism, and through my explorations I began to awaken to an alternative way of understanding our place in the world. In contrast to the freedom of "nothing," ancient religious and Indigenous cultures, from which so many of us have (often understandably) fled offer the fullness of "something." They tend to embrace the particular over the universal and the communal over the individual. They celebrate a kind of materiality that is quite the opposite of the empty, disenchanted materialism of so much of secular life. It is an enchanted materiality—one in which the whole world vibrates like a gong struck with meaning and purpose. In this worldview, everything that we do has cosmic significance.

Nefesh, Am, and Adamah

In my reading of Jewish texts as well as my own spiritual journeys, I've found that three concentric dimensions of this vibrating materiality emerge again and again: in Hebrew transliteration, they are *nefesh*, *am* (rhymes with "mom"), and *adamah*. *Nefesh* is the soul–body composite that is our human self. It is the whole of our bodies as physical manifestations of the divine. It is our sexuality and our personality, our heart and our capacity, our fingernails and the light in our eyes. *Am*, in its simplest meaning, is a community. It is not a political nation-state, nor is it necessarily restricted to a single ethnic group—indeed in the biblical exodus story, it was a "mixed multitude" that left Egypt together. It is a people, an extended family, or a joinable tribal group with a shared history and culture. *Adamah* means earth, soil, or land—the substance of the living planet herself, from which we are made and to which we return. *Adamah* is a feminine noun in Hebrew, which accords with a sense in many cultures of the earth as a maternal source of all abundance and blessings.

All three of these sacred structures—*nefesh*, *am*, and *adamah*—come up again and again in the stories of our lives and therefore the stories of this book. They are inextricable from each other. The *nefesh* is embedded in the *am*, which is embedded in the *adamah*. They are our access points to this reality we live in. It is through them that we touch into vivid joy and pain; we find meaning; we encounter other people and other beings; we connect to the past and the future; and we meet the sacred miracle that is our existence. Anything that insulates us from this direct contact insulates us from life itself. I fear that much of modern culture functions as a layer of insulation in exactly this way—it separates us from direct experience, and it dulls us. We walk around in a hazy malaise without really knowing why.

If it sounds like I am idealizing Judaism or religious traditions generally, I am probably guilty as charged. In the same way that people who feel wounded by their religious upbringing may see secularism with rose-colored glasses, I am sure that my experience of the failures of modern life blind me to some of the very real harms of traditional religious life. I am of course aware of the oppressions and violence that some religious communities have perpetrated over the years. But because I didn't grow up in such a community, I don't directly feel that pain. What's more, in every religious tradition that I know of, spiritual leaders are working to critique, reimagine, and liberate their practices. Every tradition is continuing to evolve. This is important work, and I'm glad that it's being done. But from where I sit, our society needs a different corrective most urgently right now.

What if we were to take a brief pause from critiquing ancient traditions and allow our modern selves to be critiqued by them instead? Pause from teaching from our modern perspective and try learning for a bit? Pause from reforming and be open to being reformed?

Background Grief

For eighteen years I served as a Unitarian Universalist minister, leading congregations of people, most of whom had fled their birth faiths or who, like me, never had religious community to begin with. During that time, I saw that the vague emptiness I felt as a child is not unique to me. It is chronic in our day, at least where I have the clearest window into it—among the secular professional class in wealthy nations. I see it in many of my friends as well as the people I encounter (online and otherwise) in my broader social circles. These are people whom pollsters call the "nones"— those who when asked on a survey for their religious identity check the box that says "none."

I think of Unitarian Universalists (UUs) as "nones" as well because, although some feel identified culturally with Unitarian Universalism enough to check a different box on a survey, the dynamics of their lives parallel those of their secular or "spiritual but not religious" counterparts. An old advertisement illustrates this point: "Are you a UU and don't know it?" The ability to be a UU without realizing it suggests that UUs and the "nones" often have indistinguishable worldviews, politics, and practices. It's a short trip from one to the other. Both groups tend to be well-educated, technology-loving, politically liberal, socially progressive, geographically mobile, and—certainly by global standards— wealthy. But since many people have not heard of Unitarian Universalism, many "nones" don't have a different box to check.

Unitarian Universalism has been called the quintessential American religion because its values mirror classically liberal American ideals of individualism, freedom, and a universalism that celebrates difference and diversity—especially when differences can be cast as alternative expressions of "the same" thing. For an illustration of this, consider the colorful poster that shows the Golden Rule as expressed in thirteen different religions. Unitarians and secular liberals tend to appreciate that poster because it gives a religious imprimatur to ethical beliefs. (And it suggests that we've already grasped the basic gist of religion—so we're not missing anything). This is not to suggest that UUs and secular Americans are not spiritually inclined; they are! In my experience many are craving more spirituality in their lives, not less. But free-floating spirituality unmoored from ancient religious wisdom can sometimes default to what sociologist Christian Smith describes as a diluted version of Christianity He terms it "Moralistic Therapeutic Deism (MTD)." MTD includes beliefs like, "The central goal of life is to be happy and to feel good about oneself," and, "God does not need to be particularly involved in one's life except when needed to resolve a problem." These are general liberal American ideals that, along with the capitalist ideals of meritocracy, consumerism, and now technocracy, have substituted for religiosity in the hearts of the people I have known best—my family, friends, and congregants.

As a participant-observer in this world, I have watched (and felt) the social experiment of our time play out, and I have watched (and felt) it mostly fail. In losing our grounding in ancient religious traditions, we have lost our roots, physical and spiritual, and what remains to us turns out to be inadequate to the challenges of our time or even to our private struggles. Our stock price has bottomed out just when we most need liquidity.

This is not a story that I am trained to tell in facts and statistics, although one could tell it that way. But I can tell it in the narratives of grief I have heard and lived. When all that we've lost is realized (in both senses of the word), we experience profound grief. I have born witness to this grief in my ministry and in my own heart. It is a surprising grief—even a secret grief—because it mourns the very things we felt proud to not want or need. But it is real nonetheless. I've come to hear it as a continual hum in the lives of my privileged and ostensibly thriving, happy peers: background grief.

This grief is occasioned by three intertwined types of losses. I'll call them spiritual losses, although they are fully bodily losses as well. First, the loss of the ability to fully inhabit our own *nefesh*—our spirit-soaked bodies and full-bodied souls that Walt Whitman called "the body electric": We've become alienated from our physical, animal nature. We shape and use our bodies as vehicles for our personal aspirations. We overmedicate and over-beautify. We rage against all bodily limitations, as we rage against the limits of the earth. We fight against the signs of aging and consider death a defeat to be avoided at all costs. We cede our bodies' innate childbirth wisdom to experts. Today's account of gender unmoors our selfhood from our sexed bodies. And we ignore bodies altogether as we exist increasingly in virtual spaces.

Second, loss of the *am*—relationship with one another: In our increasingly virtual and polarized social media world, we are losing our appetite for connecting face-to-face with other human beings. We are increasingly living alone, working from home, dating less, marrying less, and having less sex and fewer children. As the fabric of our social world frays and our social confidence declines, we compensate by commodifying our relationships. We outsource to professionals services as intimate as visiting grandparents or setting up a romantic scene for a marriage proposal, complete with rose petals and champagne. For twenty-five dollars an hour we can even "Rent a Pal"—a friendly person to accompany us to events or just take a walk. (The advertising reads, "No need to feel alone when you can have somebody at your side!") We do not know who "our people" are, and in-person community is becoming harder and harder to find.

Third, loss of relationship with the *adamah*, the earth: We are not "from" anywhere—we have no connection to land or any particular spot on earth. We do not know where our food comes from or whence water flows to our tap. We estrange our sibling creatures for use as "resources." We do not accept our place in the sacred web of life, and so we engage in mindless consumption. We try to shield our eyes from the sight of the cruelty and desecration perpetuated in our name. As mammals, we can sense the dissolving of the natural world around us and the impending danger, but we don't know how to place the feeling of foreboding and sadness. It seems like strawberries get less flavorful every year, but we can't remember what they used to taste like.

I've come to see these three losses as both cause and effect of our modern predicament, inextricably intertwined with our collective retreat from religious life. We lack a shared heritage of stories and a community of faith to support our soul's journey. We have a tasting platter of new do-it-yourself rituals before us but no time-tested wisdom path or spiritual technologies to cultivate our communities. And we have no ancestral teachings of how to live in and with the land. What's lost, then, is our ability to fully receive the sacred gifts of life that we have been given: the natural world and our physical incarnation within it.

There are no easy solutions to all this because there is no "bad guy." There is no single individual or even institutional culprit that could be identified and swapped out for someone or something better. The changes our societies have undergone are so profound and all-encompassing that their tentacles touch every part of the world and every aspect of our lives. Their ideologies are deeply embedded in our financial systems, food systems, histories, health, and relationships, all of which reinforce each other. Where religious practices have receded, products and services born of corporate capitalism have interpolated themselves between us and the world. Further complicating matters, they are not all harmful—humans have enjoyed many benefits from the freedoms and advances of our era. And most confounding of all is that every one of us participates daily in the practices and discourse that keep the whole system aloft. *We* are the ones who reproduce it and sustain it.

Albert Einstein was reputed to have said, "If I were given an hour to solve a problem and my life depended on solving it, I would spend fifty-five minutes understanding the problem and five minutes thinking about a solution." *The Secret Despair of the Secular Left* is the "fifty-five minutes" understanding the problem.

It is an exploration of the bodily, relational, and ecological losses suffered in modern society, told through what I have come to understand as stories of grief. It is an examination of how the different types of losses interpenetrate and connect to each other in surprising ways. Some are stories of my friends and former congregants (with identifying information removed); some are my own stories; and some are those of the public proponents of secular triumphalism and the meritocracy. It is my hope that these narratives will shed light on something invisible because of its ubiquity and something painful to which we have become numb.

I have tried to also include some of the "five minutes," in the form of religious teachings that guide me, mystical insights that inspire me, and accounts of how I and others have intentionally tried to reinvest in the things that matter most. I am awed by the natural power of regeneration that's available when we invoke it—how ecosystems rush to heal and surge back into abundance if given the slightest opening, how teenagers relearn how to communicate with others when they turn off their phones for just a week. I try to share some of that awe in these pages. My intention is to tell all of these stories, even the most difficult ones, in service of a collective return to real life, regrounding in the gifts of *nefesh*, *am*, and *adamah*.

False Consciousness

I want to concede that many people, even most people I know among the secular left, may describe themselves as happy with their choices. Many have told me directly that they are happy, certainly happier than when they were, say, religious as children. To the extent that they are unhappy with their lives in general, they attribute that unhappiness to other factors. So in writing about the grief and despair that I've witnessed, it may be that I am unfairly accusing people of false consciousness. I should never presume to know what is inside the heart or mind of another.

For many people disillusioned with or disinterested in religion, what they have found in its stead, be it a religion substitute, a political movement, or identity-based affiliation, has provided an invaluable source of meaning and connection. It's not my place to discount people's positive experience. And after all, is there really any difference between thinking you're happy and actually being happy?

But what I am describing in these pages is a sense, when I look around, of *collective* trauma—not carried by any one person or group who is "doing it wrong." When people tell me their individual stories of despair, it feels like the separate stories are often traceable to common sources. Many of my own painful stories are traceable to those same sources. I see signs that our experiences of disembodiment, disconnection, and dislocation in secular modernity have generated a trauma field—a shared space of grief in which we have collectively compensated by creating new social and material realities. Within the matrix of these new realities, we may feel happy. But it seems that the bar has been lowered so far that we can no longer even imagine what it might feel like to live expansive spiritual lives rooted in our bodies, multigenerational communities, and the earth.

Here's an example: Because in the modern era so many of us have started to leave the land and home of our birth, our collective consciousness created Zoom. Videoconferencing allowed us to stay in touch from afar. This eased the pain of separation and probably accelerated the process of local communities breaking apart. (In fact, research has shown that white-collar workers who can work remotely now live twice as far from their workplaces as they did pre-pandemic.) Virtual modalities soon became so central to our communication that regardless of where we live, if we don't have something like Zoom or, God forbid, don't have a computing device on which to run it, we are unable to function in society.

Of course, to have a computing device is to also have a bank account, credit card, and email address and to make enough money to keep paying for services and buying new devices as the old become unusable. It is to be locked into a profound entanglement in the financial and technological systems of our society. Only people who are homeless or otherwise living on the fringes of society are deprived of these things (if you try to forgo them, you may well end up impoverished as well, if you weren't already). And so, *in comparison to the alternative* of complete estrangement, our virtual connections can seem perfectly satisfactory. We humans are adept at making the most of what is rather than wallowing in what could be, should be, or once was.

But that doesn't mean that nothing real has been lost; in fact, it may mean that what has been lost is so huge, we can't even see it. In the example above, the geographical *dislocation* leads to the relational *disconnection* which leads to the *disembodiment* of online living. And the online living, in turn, feeds the process of dislocation. It's all of a piece; each loss reinforces the other. The virtual world becomes part of an invisible latticework of compensatory social agreements, ideologies, and numbness generated by the trauma we've all suffered.

It is in the context of this invisible latticework that today's forms of traditionalism and religiosity are forced to eke out an existence, either as resistance or as a humorless, dry legalism—a desperate attempt to codify traditional lifeways before they disappear altogether. But the result is often a strangled, artificial form of these traditional lifeways. The remaining people who practice them are an embattled minority who can come across as downright bizarre. Small wonder that these paths seem unappealing or even oppressive to many modern people. Alternatively, some religious movements have responded to religion's decline by watering themselves down, becoming tepid and apologetic in order to not scare people off by broadcasting too much difference or imposing too many demands. Any rules, commandments, or norms come to seem burdensome. This approach also backfires, and the pews continue to empty.

In thinking about collective trauma, I'm inspired by the work of Thomas Hübl, who writes and teaches about how everything that happens to us as individuals happens collectively, and vice versa. Together we create energetic patterns that emerge as fractals. He writes:

> The collective body-mind—the part of us that is vastly and mystifyingly connected—is traumatized and therefore greatly fragmented, disconnected, polarized, and separated. Why? From a mystical perspective, every systemic and seemingly intractable social problem, regardless of where it plays out in the world, springs from the same source: the deep, compounding unhealed morass of humanity's unresolved past. . . . For evidence of incoherence and fragmentation, we need only consider the degree to which either *hyper*-arousal (e.g. social anxiety, intensity, distrust, agitation, fear, aggression) or *hypo*-arousal (e.g. numbing, apathy, lethargy, disconnection, ennui, pessimism) is present. We might think of these phenomena as the "check engine" light of culture.

Today in our society we see plenty of both hyper-arousal and hypo-arousal, even among the young left-leaning set who claim to be reclaiming meaning, pleasure, and power in new, progressive modalities. In fact, in a somewhat embarrassing phenomenon, five decades of sociological research has consistently shown that conservatives are happier than liberals. There are many different theories to explain this, ranging from "conservatives are more likely to be married, and marriage makes people happy" to "conservatives are more likely to be religious, and religion makes people happy." But whatever the explanation, the finding holds true across demographic and even national borders. Incidentally, conservatives also have more children, give more to charity, and vote more reliably when it's raining. It seems that some unrealized loss in secular culture is very quietly draining our lives of enthusiasm and commitment.

What to Do with a Rosary

A friend of mine shared a story with me from her summer working as an intern chaplain at a hospital: On this particular day she was working in the ER, and a patient was brought in who was freshly injured and very upset. He was belligerent—yelling and struggling. His wounds got treated, and eventually he calmed down enough that my friend could talk with him. She listened to his story, and as he told it a great sadness fell over him. Finally he said, "I know what I need. I need a rosary. I need to pray the rosary. Do you guys have a rosary here?"

A rosary is a string of beads used as a Catholic prayer tool. The supplicant recites a particular prayer for each bead or set of beads and moves along the whole loop, cycling through several different prayers. I imagine that, as with most spiritual technologies, you have to do this a lot before it becomes second nature and you can really sink into it as a meditative, devotional practice. So the patient wanted a rosary, and my friend knew that the chaplain's office did, in fact, have some plastic rosaries available. So she went in search of a rosary, found it, returned a few minutes later, and handed it to him. He took it and stared at her blankly. He asked, "Now what do I do?"

The poor guy had to find out the hard way that the time to learn how to pray the rosary is not when you're in crisis; it's long before. My friend guessed that he had been raised Catholic but hadn't engaged with it for years, probably because it hadn't felt necessary and he preferred to spend his time in other ways. But a spiritual practice is an investment, and like any good investment, it starts small and its value grows over time. Then it's there when you need it. So many things are like this. Lifelong New Yorkers like to say that the best way to be able to afford an apartment in Manhattan is to have bought it forty years ago. The best time to plant a tree is also forty years ago. The best time to learn to play violin or speak Mandarin: long ago. We have to invest before we need it, whatever it is—the practice, the apartment, the tree—and before there's much payoff. The patient had not made that investment, and now he was bereft.

Many of us these days, including me, are like that patient. Whether because of the distractions of modern life or negative experiences with our birth traditions (or simply no experiences), we were not able to get in at the ground floor and buy our stock early. When trouble hits—as it inevitably does—we have a vague sense that there's something out there that could help, and that that "something" has something to do with religion and spirituality, community and tradition. But we don't know how to access it. We peer in through the window and often give up and walk away.

When I was a child, although my family was not religious, I was fascinated by the idea of religion. I visited churches and synagogues every weekend, pressing my nose against the glass. The assistant pastor at a local Presbyterian church offered to discuss the Bible with me. So I went every week, telling myself that I was just intellectually curious about this opiate of the masses. But underneath my cool remove was a yearning for the rituals, disciplines, practices, and mysteries of religious life. I was fascinated by the stories. I fantasized about becoming a nun. I imagined even that being a clergy person would be a great career for me. This kindly pastor's job seemed ideal. It was really too bad I didn't have a religion, I thought to myself.

For years after that, my spiritual search went dormant. I flailed around in college, with no real career ambitions. I eventually circled back to religious exploration through Eastern spirituality. I explored Buddhist meditation, traveled to India, and became enamored with Hinduism through yoga and Hindu philosophy. Where previously I had thought of religious concerns as heady and ethereal, yogic practice presupposed a spiritual energy whose free flow or constriction manifested in the body.

I was in my early twenties when I learned that I was Jewish. I heard almost an audible "click" as a puzzle piece fell into place. It made some sense of me to myself that I couldn't quite put a finger on. At the time, I didn't do much with the information but tucked it away. It was just a fun fact. It was simply something lost that I never had to begin with.

But as the years went by, I kept finding myself drawn to religious life, especially to synagogues and Jewish learning. I began to realize that I was heir to a gorgeous tradition of spiritual practices, rituals, music, and texts, dazzling in their breadth and depth. As I read and learned more, I fell in love with it. I found that as you drill down into any prayer, practice, or Hebrew word, it opens up like a geode into a cavernous, glowing space with layers of spiritual meanings and passageways to yet more gems. Far from the oppressive power that my parents and peers felt it was, I began to think of Jewish tradition and ancient religious traditions generally as oases of nourishment and radical countercultural fire. Here were the antidotes to the pain of modernity, right under our noses. Here were the bodily practices, the communal superglue, and the ecological teachings whose absence was sending us all into a global tailspin.

My desire to live in the religious world as a clergy person came rushing back. The rabbinate seemed out of reach for the time being—among other limitations, I didn't yet read Hebrew. As strangely familiar as Jewish spirituality felt, it also still felt foreign. I was like the ER patient who had asked for the rosary but didn't know how to use it. So I joined Unitarian Universalism as a carpetbagger. In a way it was a natural fit: this was the religi-fied version of my upbringing. Creedless and rule-less, its principles were innocuous, with lots of freedom to shape them as I pleased. And the people were kind and sincere. I studied, received my MDiv degree, and got ordained as a UU minister. I began serving congregations in the Chicago area and then in New York City. Having not been a UU before beginning this career, I learned on the job. And my Jewish journey continued apace.

For years I attended Jewish Renewal services on Saturday mornings and led UU services on Sunday mornings. To experience the contrast week after week was an invaluable education. With secular values earnestly cast as "religious" in the UU world, I got a rare window into the theology underpinning those values. It took years before I finally felt ready, but in 2020 I enrolled in rabbinical school, part-time, through the Jewish Renewal's Aleph Ordination Program. I simultaneously continued my career as a UU minister for four more years. The insights I gained through almost two decades living this odd double life animate this book.

Surplus Grief in Modern Death

Early in my ministry, when I was serving a Unitarian Universalist congregation in the Midwest, I was called for an urgent pastoral visit with a congregant, Clara, whose husband had suffered a cardiac arrest the night before. When I arrived at the hospital, he was unconscious and intubated, and I sat with Clara in the visitor lounge. Pale and shuddering, she caught me up on everything that had happened. The doctors had done everything they could, but her husband had no realistic chance of recovery. The decision had been made to take him off life support. She was in shock, but she understood and accepted this decision. Then she said something that has haunted me all the years since: "I'm not supposed to be in his room when it happens."

She explained that the doctors had told her that once they "pulled the plug" it might well take some time for him to die, and it would be too hard to watch. So she shouldn't be there. And they assured her that he was not aware of anything anyway. I was appalled by this advice and equally appalled that she was ready to take it. But I immediately saw that I had no authority in this domain. As a Unitarian Universalist minister, I represented a movement without a shared code of religious ethics and without traditions around death and dying. There were no obligations of care to point to, no theology of a soul's journey, no collective faith in a consciousness that transcends the brain, which, in this man's case, had flatlined. I had no religious grounds on which to tell Clara that she ought to be with her husband, holding his hand as he dies. That was simply my personal opinion, which I had not been invited to share.

And so I fell back, in my professional role, on a principle that I knew *did* have weight in the secular ethic: that of personal choice and rights. I reminded Clara that whether or not to be in her husband's room was her decision to make—not the doctors'. I asked her what she wanted. Did she *want* to be with him when he died? She seemed confused and distressed by this question and the subtle implied nudge. "I don't know. I don't think so. I mean, they're the experts. They're probably right. It probably would be too hard to watch." Watching her quavering uncertainty, her groping for guidance, I was struck by how little Clara had to fall back on—neither the external structure of religious tradition nor the internal compass calibrated through religious practice.

I held back the next question that was on the tip of my tongue: "What do you think *he* would want?" Instead, I offered her an alternative that, to my thinking, was a distant second best: "Would you like me to go in and sit with him?" She nodded and burst into tears of gratitude and relief.

And so it was that Clara went home, and I ended up sitting by the bedside, holding the hand of a complete stranger as he gradually died over the next several hours. The nurses came in periodically to check on us and gave him increasing doses of morphine, ostensibly for pain but clearly, also, to move the process along. When he died, I was struck anew at how palpably, unmistakably different a dead man is from an unconscious one. I left the hospital, called Clara, and let her know.

Don't Judge and Never Guilt

When I got back to the church, I recounted what had happened to my supervisor, the senior minister of the congregation. He must have sensed my discomfort with how it had played out, and he assured me that I had done the right thing. "The most important thing," he said, "is to never make them feel guilty." He saw it as a kindness and indeed a professional pastoral obligation to support Clara's belief that she had made the right choice. If there is one cardinal rule in liberal religious and secular leadership, it is this principle: Never make them feel guilty; never make them feel judged. By extension, never push them to do something hard, like sit with a suffering loved one as they die, because if they prove unable to do it, then they may feel guilty. And it should be their choice, after all.

If clergy are supposed to be spiritual guides, avoiding the imposition of guilt is a tricky maneuver, especially when the never-guilt value is paired with the absolute-personal-choice value. When people have complete freedom to choose and must never be made to feel that they chose "wrong," then any choice they could make has to be deemed equally right. The clergy role—and the role of religious community—becomes purely about affirmation. In effect, right and wrong, virtue and sin are erased from the equation—except in a scenario of direct harm to someone else, which even the most libertarian among us will still admit as a wrong. Outside of that narrow exception, we operate with a practical philosophy of moral relativism.

I say "practical" philosophy because I think if you asked most people if they are moral relativists, they would say no. In theory, people believe in the concept of right and wrong. People affirm that we have obligations to each other and maybe even to the earth herself. But what good are abstract principles of right and wrong if every particular act is ruled out of bounds for moral evaluation? What good are *mitzvot*—commandments—if everyone knows we're not really expected to keep them if we don't want to? When you get out of the theoretical clouds and down to practical reality—the nitty gritty of someone else's choices—we tend to retreat. We decline the unsavory task of sorting right from wrong and instead fall back on the don't-judge-and-never-guilt ethic.

There is good reason for this aversion to guilt. Guilt has been weaponized and used as a tool of control by religious authorities for eons. By labeling as "sin" universal human experiences like sexual desire or masturbation, everyone is guilty and everyone is spiritually in arrears, indebted to the clergy or to God as mediated by the religious institution. When inflicted to maintain power, guilt becomes toxic. I wasn't raised with this kind of religiously weaponized guilt (though I was served guilt, God-free), so it's hard for me to fully understand what that's like. But many of my congregants had experienced it, and now any hint of guilt language can trigger painful memories and anger. As adults, some were still reeling from the trauma it inflicted.

It might seem overblown to use the word "trauma" to describe feeling judged for our infractions. But in the stories that my congregants told, the guilt imposed by religious authorities morphed into shame, which is a very different animal. Rather than aiming to critique a particular act, shame critiques a person's very selfhood. Professor of social work Dr. Brené Brown defines shame as "the intensely painful feeling or experience of believing that we are flawed and therefore unworthy of love or belonging." So, far beyond "this action was wrong," it's "I am bad." And we've seen that in some communities, shame is meted out asymmetrically, with women and gender minorities bearing the brunt of punishment for just being human.

Guilt and shame have been primary drivers of the flight from religious life in the modern era. Indeed, why would anyone want to be part of a system that produces so much pain? Religious institutions have often botched the handling of this problem. Millions of people over the span of a single generation dropped their religious affiliations like hot potatoes, and with it any tolerance for anything with even the slightest whiff of potentially guilt-inducing religious obligation. In the process they lost so much that could have supported and sustained them through their lives. In allowing guilt to breed shame, and conflating wrong actions with unworthy personhood, religious institutions have failed us.

Limited Liability Clause

When a religious community is doing its job right, it offers its members a limited liability clause—you can never do something so bad that your soul faces annihilation. It holds solid the line between guilt and shame—reinforces it with steel girders and a wall of fire—and never, ever crosses over to the shame side. To the contrary, where shame tells us we are ontologically rotten to the core, religious teachings should align with spiritual revelation: that our glowing core is untouchable—pure goodness and love. We each have a spark of the divine within us. This core may get obscured or even distorted by our actions, but nothing and no one can take it away from us. We are made in the image of a plural God (who speaks in the Genesis text, "let us make an earthling in our image"), and there are plural ways of expressing holiness in this world. Nothing can possibly make us unworthy of God's love, which is infinite and unconditional.

A healthy religious community acknowledges and normalizes the idea that we humans make mistakes. It wears no rose-colored glasses. We do things that are ethically wrong, hurtful, emotionally unskillful, and harm people or other living beings, unintentionally and sometimes intentionally. When we do this—not if, but when—it's natural to feel badly about it, even guilty.

Religious teachings can give us language and a container for this feeling. They can help us clarify the difference in our own hearts between doing something wrong and being a bad or unworthy person. They allow us to see what we did wrong in the context of everyone else who has ever done anything wrong. Rituals give us a path toward fixing it—with God, in our own hearts, and sometimes—blessedly—with the people we have hurt. In Jewish tradition, this process is called *teshuvah*, which means turning or returning back to spiritual alignment. Most religious traditions offer spiritual technologies for this kind of return. The Jewish High Holidays, Lent, and Ramadan all offer pathways for return. This recurring motion of return is a primal gesture of religious life. It is also central to the practice of meditation in which, as our attention naturally strays, we return to the breath, the deeper Self, or the meditative consciousness over and over again.

Knowing that there is a structure and a process for *teshuvah* can be enormously liberating. We can take bold actions, walking out on the tightrope of the world, knowing that there's a safety net underneath. If we fall, that is, if we do something wrong, we will not fall to the ground. We will be caught. We will still be worthy of love. We will be able to make amends, at least with God if not with whomever we may have wronged. Once this is in place, then we can be supported and even pushed to do the right thing even if, like going out on the high wire, it's scary or difficult. I wish that Clara had had such a structure in place and could have gone out on the high wire in the hospital that day.

Death and Dying

I was glad I had been able to help Clara in the moment. But I also felt deflated—sad for her and for her husband and sad for this lonely, confused world we've built. Clara had substituted a professional service (mine) for what could have been her final private gift to her husband. She may or may not have been spared guilt in his last hours, but I fear that her grief was ultimately amplified. Her overflowing gratitude at my offer to sit with him revealed what was true in her heart—she knew that he shouldn't die alone, despite what the doctors said. She probably also knew that he shouldn't die with a stranger who was essentially paid to be there. But as a secular liberal, she had no spiritual framework for the significance of this moment, no traditions to hold her up, no mythic stories to mirror her own. In me, her minister, she had plenty of support to do what she wanted to do but no support to do the right, though hard, thing.

Had Clara been part of a mature religious community, this might have played out quite differently. She could have had two supports: (1) the support of clergy encouraging her to do the right thing, and (2) the support of a structure where she would know what to do—songs to sing, steps to take. She could have come out of this situation knowing that she gave her beloved a final gift and acted compassionately and honorably. And her husband could have been accompanied in his transition by his wife instead of a stranger.

While in most traditions there is no absolute requirement to be present at the moment of death (because it's not always possible), it is assumed that every effort will be made to accompany the dying on their final journey. It is considered a matter of respect, at the very least, to watch over someone as they make the awesome transition from this world to the next. Each tradition offers robust spiritual practices for the dying person and the family at this vivid and often painful time. In some traditions the dying person, if they can speak, recites specific prayers, makes confessions, asks and offers forgiveness. Some have a word for this phase of active dying (in Hebrew, *goses*). The family may recite prayers, chant, give to charity, and tend to the physical suffering of their loved one. Even after death, in some traditions the body of the deceased is never to be left alone but is always accompanied with prayers and psalms until burial.

Transcendent Consciousness

Undergirding these practices are theologies of both the sacredness of the body and the presence of a soul or transcendent consciousness. Together these concepts point to a holistic understanding of a human being made in the image of the divine. They honor the body as not just a shell or vehicle for the self, but as the physical dimension of the person. Jewish morning prayers include gratitude for the power of healing and the body as a whole that is wondrously made. This reverence for the physical body expresses what biblical scholar Ellen Davis calls a "wholesome materiality" that extends to the physical world in general. The body and the physical world are not merely resources to be shaped, used, and used up. They are the sacred elements that constitute the substance of creation.

At the same time, many religious traditions teach of a consciousness that transcends this plane of existence. We hear tell of this consciousness in the mystical poems and songs, in people's near-death experiences across cultures and generations, and in the teachings and stories of the soul in sacred texts. Most importantly, we experience it ourselves, *in* ourselves—the spirit or selfhood that is more than the sum of our parts. We know in our hearts that we are more than just complex machines.

Researchers in artificial intelligence are working busily to disprove this idea. They posit that if they give a computer enough data, sensory-mimicking inputs, and learning programs, the machine will someday spontaneously generate consciousness. Or at least, its ability to converse and create will be indistinguishable from that of humans. If that's not "real" consciousness, they argue, then perhaps human consciousness is not real either. Perhaps every word we speak and every emotion we feel is just the output stream of a giant algorithm. One serious theory holds that we have the internal experience of "consciousness" not because we are conscious, but because that feeling produces an evolutionary advantage, if only because it gives us more motivation to stay alive.

In one of the evolving triumphs of today's AI research, computers are now able to generate convincing images of people who never existed. You can test yourself online and guess which one of two side-by-side photos is an image of a real person and which one was generated by AI (a kind of visual Turing test). A rabbi friend of mine tried this and was deeply distressed that he was unable to tell the difference. What kind of rabbi was he that he couldn't tell the difference between a real person and a fake?!

Another way to look at his confusion, however, is not that it proves the genius of AI as much as it reveals the poverty of digital images. A digital image of a person is two-dimensional, literally and figuratively. The spacious soul and the life force are not there; the constantly shifting tides of a human being are not there. It is frozen in time, ossified. It is not surprising that this is indistinguishable from an AI-generated image. There is something sacred in the presence of a human (or other animal) that is absent in *any* digital image. It's the difference I sensed in Clara's husband, though he was perfectly still, when he passed from life to death.

It is today's reductionist, tech-warped worldview that underlies a doctor's recommendation that one not be present with an unconscious patient. And this worldview, when suggested to a vulnerable, frightened family member with no counterpoint spiritual language, can bring a surfeit of grief. If love dies with the body, our isolation is absolute; our loneliness is profound. It does not have to be this way. But for it to be otherwise—to have a rooted faith strong enough to uphold us when crisis arrives—requires a significant investment in the spiritual teachings, language, stories, and practices of a faith tradition—and in the work of cultivating faith itself.

The Secular Gaze

Feminist theorists in the 1970s coined the term "the male gaze" to describe the way women were evaluated and culturally constructed through a masculine way of seeing the world. In a similar way, religious cultures today are evaluated and constructed through a secular way of seeing. The secular gaze has become the norm and the default (coded masculine). The religious community is the "other" (coded feminine). The burden of proof is on the religious community to demonstrate its value and minimize its impact on the wider society.

David, a former congregant who had moved out of the city years ago, called me at the church wanting to discuss plans for a memorial service for his wife, whose death was imminent. He planned to have her body cremated and to sprinkle the ashes in various places where they had shared memories. The memorial at the church would serve as a celebration of her life at a later date when it was convenient for relatives to come to town. In the course of our conversation, it came out that he was uneasy with the decision to cremate her body. David was a lapsed Catholic and had powerful memories of attending his grandfather's funeral, visiting his grandfather's grave, maintaining the headstone, and bringing flowers every year, even when the rest of his family had long neglected it. He was tempted to inter his wife's body in accordance with this tradition. Additionally, his wife was Jewish, and she had on at least one occasion mentioned that she would like to be buried, not cremated, as is also required by Jewish law.

Cremation and Secular Neutrality

The crematorium is the most popular destination for dead bodies in the United States and only becoming more so. It has become the standard, especially for educated liberals like David. So despite the quiet tug he was feeling on his heart, the secular norm of cremation won the day. As a nonreligious thinker confronted with metaphysical questions, he floundered. He had few tools at his disposal to help him understand the dynamics at play here. He, like so many of us, defaulted to a straightforward, secular logic: Cremation is less expensive than burial, and to modern sensibilities it feels "cleaner," more genteel. The waterlogged messiness of the body is expunged. There are no smelly bodily fluids and no process of early decomposition to contend with. After cremation, we are dry and sterile. (Of course, the process of embalming also denies the body's disintegration, but it doesn't try to disappear the body.) With cremation, most of the evidence of the body vanishes, although there are often bone fragments left among the ashes. This fits well with the modern account of the body as merely a vehicle for the self. Once the body is dead, we should not care what happens to it because the person is believed to be no longer there.

This belief runs counter to the intuition that many of us have that in fact an important facet of the person *is* there.

Yes, in religious terms we are more than material beings, but the spiritual liquidation of the self after death is a mysterious process, which we cannot fully understand or rush. In Tibetan Buddhist circles, spiritual adepts will sometimes at the time of death enter the state of *tukdam*—their bodies are clinically dead but remain seated in meditation, without rigor mortis and without decay, sometimes for weeks. It is believed that they are resting in deep meditative consciousness. In Hindu tradition bodies are cremated, but only after a home funeral with the body present, and generally as part of a public ritual at a funeral pyre intended to aid the soul's release from the body.

There is no bright line between spirit and matter. When we try to discipline and direct our mourning to what we think is its proper object (i.e., the abstract "person" or—better yet in modern parlance—the "memory"), we deny something vital in our humanity. But deny it we do. The authority of secular ideology is so powerful it seems to easily override not only religious authority but also our nagging, holy feelings of discomfort. I'm thinking of people like David who wanted to bury his wife's body but didn't, and people like Clara who knew that she should hold her husband's hand while he died but didn't. They capitulated to powerful social norms over the clamor of an internal protest that they could barely hear. Even when I or someone else tries to hold a microphone to that internal protest for them, it remains almost inaudible.

For people without a religious or spiritual grounding, this process tends to go unacknowledged. Something as commonplace as cremation can come packaged with a full-fledged ideology of the body and personhood, but we are never asked whether we buy into this ideology. It's hard to grasp what's at stake in these decisions, and when we are already in a moment of crisis it's never the right time to figure it out. The secular worldview swoops into the breach at the moment of vulnerability and provides a quick and easy solution. In this case, no one in particular is profiting from one choice over the other, and there is certainly no intentional conspiracy at work. But a soulless economic system sustains itself generally by severing our connections with our traditions, our bodies, our communities, and the earth.

The Secular Path Disguised as No Path

That the ideological content of a practice like cremation remains invisible to so many of its modern practitioners is, in my view, one of the strongest cases for religious education. By "religious education," I mean broadly the transmission and integration of the entire matrix of spiritual practices, intellectual learning, ritual, and communal life that comprise a tradition. When a child's or adult's growth is supported by such an education, they gain both language and permission for more-than-rational ways of knowing. They may develop a political consciousness seated in ideals outside of the ordinary spectrum of liberal versus conservative options. And they can gain tools of spiritual discernment—a way of seeing the world that equips them to understand more of what's at stake in the everyday decisions of our lives.

Our secular cultural institutions from public schools to museums to news media enjoy the conceit that what they offer is neutrality, like the so-called "nothingness" of my childhood home—just bland administrative containers for the blooming of a thousand flowers. But where the secular mind sees neutrality and even-handedness, the religious mind can often detect a specific theology (a theology of personhood embedded in the practice of cremation, for example). A person who journeys down a particular religious and spiritual path can readily recognize a different path when they see it, even when it's disguised as no path at all.

Having once believed in the neutrality of the secular worldview myself, I used to share my liberal peers' horror at any religious intrusions on public life. I believed that the separation of church and state was important in order to protect "state" (representing the universal) from the incursions of "church" (representing the particular). And I still believe this separation can be useful in, for example, avoiding a Christian theocracy in the United States. But as I became more religious myself over the years and particularly once I had children, I began to see the larger issues somewhat differently.

For their preschool year, my children went to a Jewish day school in Manhattan. They loved it, and we, their parents, loved it. I was amazed at how the children were reading and writing in English and Hebrew, as well as learning about Torah stories and holidays. At this school it was assumed that all the families kept Shabbat—a time focused on gratitude for all that we have and are. Children would help bake challahs on Friday and get out early from school so their families could get ready for the weekly holiday. I was especially moved by how these 4-year-olds and their teachers would talk in depth about Jewish values. I remember once hearing of a conversation about poverty in which—in addition to a lesson about *tzedakah* (justice-charity)—the children were asked to discuss the difference between their wants and their needs. My daughter, Miriam, later used the framework she had learned in that conversation in a real-life situation where she explained that she *wanted* something but also volunteered that she did not *need* it.

For financial reasons, the following year we decided to enroll the children in the local public elementary school. It was considered one of the best public elementary schools in the city, it was right in our neighborhood, and it was free. They have continued in New York City's public school system ever since, and we have found much to appreciate about it—the greater cultural diversity is a gift, the academics have been rigorous enough, and the kids have friends and generally look forward to going to school. Values, however, are meant to be handled on our own time. (An exception to this rule is the teaching of values around multiculturalism and sexual and gender diversity, which are considered noncontroversial, neutral values in the liberal milieus of our children's schools.)

There is no special regard for the religious observances of the few students who have them. Religion is treated like a hobby, sport, or other extracurricular activity—something appended to a "normal" life, which is secular. A case in point: When Miriam started middle school, we were delighted to discover that there were a variety of after-school activities the students could choose to do. She wanted to try debate, which was a club (and everyday activity) that I had enjoyed as a teen. We read the information—it met once a week after school, and it looked just right for her. We signed her up for it, and she began it. All was well until we received an email letting us know that debate competitions would be taking place on Saturdays (in other words, Shabbat), on Zoom. The email assured us that the competitions were optional.

This immediately precipitated a conflict in our family. We are committed to a Shabbat practice of non-striving— enjoying the abundance of all that we already have. Each week, for the twenty-five hours of the holiday, we aspire to enter a timeless, noncompetitive state without alarms, screens, and to-do lists in which we can be together, be in nature as much as our urban existence allows, and rest in the faith that we have done enough for the week. Even though it would not be "work" in the conventional sense, a debate competition felt antithetical to the spirit of Shabbat that we were cultivating.

But understandably, Miriam did not want to be left out of what we now understood was an important component of the debate program. All of her peers would be doing it. Besides, she argued, she *wanted* to debate in these competitions and would enjoy doing it. This would not feel like work. Shouldn't Shabbat be about doing what we *want*? Here the unassailable secular logic had crept into our Jewish family life. I know that the debate competition is what you *want*, I wanted to say, but Shabbat is what you *need*. I knew this reasoning would fall flat. The religious perspective that my husband and I offered felt frail and isolated, surrounded on all sides by society's towering confidence in freedom, choice, and the fulfillment of individual desires.

Declaring the competitions to be optional exonerated the public school from any responsibility for impinging on religious freedom. The state has no interest in what a child or family decides, as long as there is no direct coercion involved. But here too this administrative neutrality masks an overpowering gravitational pull toward the secular worldview. The peer pressure for young people is intense (as everyone knows), and adult role models in the faculty often show their anti-religious biases as well. When my daughter talked with her debate club teacher about the Shabbat issue, rather than showing support for her family's religious commitments, the teacher commiserated with her, saying, "That really stinks."

And so the battle lines get drawn. The state—in this case represented by the public school—formally accommodates religious practice by making the Saturday debates optional and so becomes the "nice" parent, offering the kids whatever they want. The family and the religion become the "mean" parent, offering something that by contrast feels austere and parsimonious. At our kids' Jewish day school, of course, Shabbat felt anything but austere and parsimonious. It was joyful and fun. It was a time everyone looked forward to. But now a shadow had been cast over the practice of Shabbat. And once this happens, in my experience, there is no going back. The secular world has triumphed simply by planting a seed of resentment in the child.

The Third Framework

To be clear, there is no malice in these policies. No one is scheming in a smoky back room somewhere to destroy the faith of children. There is, at worst, an assumption about the inherent superiority of secular ideology to religious ideology. There is an attempt to be even-handed to religious and nonreligious children while at the same time ensuring that religious practices never impinge on "normal" activities.

But in a conflict like this one, secularism effectively swings the frame of reference so that rather than a religious perspective serving as the orienting framework through which the child understands the world, there are now two competing frameworks—that of secular norms versus that of religious commitments. Whenever there are two competing frameworks, a *third framework* has to come into play to adjudicate between the two. In our society, that third framework invariably turns out to be some form of assessment of what the individual wants, what would feel liberating, what would help them advance in the meritocracy, what would be "healthy" according to contemporary psychology, what would be a moderate position between extremes, or what would be "normal." In other words, the third framework is merely the secular framework recapitulated. And so the end result of these well-meaning and supposedly unbiased priorities of the public schools is a quiet thumb on the scale in favor of secular culture.

This quiet thumb on the scale is the secular gaze, and it pervades all our social institutions. Public swimming pools offer another case study. In Orthodox Jewish tradition, women do not dress immodestly (including wearing swimsuits) in front of men. This religious requirement means that public swimming pools across the country are off limits to women unless the pool hosts women-only swimming hours. In Brooklyn's heavily Orthodox Crown Heights and Williamsburg neighborhoods, public pools have done just that—offered a few hours a week when only women may swim. This humane policy has provoked outrage and condemnation from the Human Rights Commission and the ACLU on the basis of purported gender discrimination. The *New York Times* editorial board joined with LGBTQ+ activists in opposing the policy on the grounds that it reifies the gender binary.

In 2016, the Parks Department temporarily suspended the women-only hours after an anonymous complaint prompted an investigation, which found that, indeed, the policy was in violation of the city's human rights law. The hours were reinstated after some political wrangling, but today the issue is still a matter of contention, resulting in very few hours when Orthodox women can swim. The demand for these hours far outstrips the supply, and women complain that the overcrowding creates a safety hazard. One explained that she had to stop bringing her elderly mother to swim for fear that she would get hurt. Such is the power of the "third framework," this time in the form of a concern for human rights.

In learning about this controversy, I was struck by the intensity of the outrage and the strength of the backlash on the part of the secular community. When asked to make a small sacrifice for the sake of the religious commitments of others—a blink in the secular gaze—some experienced it as an assault on their rights. I suspect that if the reason for ceding a few hours a week of open swim time had been something they could relate to—like children's swim lessons or designated time for people with disabilities—it would not have provoked their ire in the same way. Religion is understood to be "elective" in a way that childhood and disability are not. In our consumer culture, religion is simply one of many market choices, like the choice of breakfast cereal—some people like some kinds, others like other kinds, and some don't like cereal at all. Certainly no one should be forced to make any concessions to facilitate someone else's breakfast preferences.

Additionally, among many secular progressives I have known, there is a negative judgment about the particular breakfast cereal eaten by conservative and orthodox religious people. Rules around modesty are seen as oppressive artifacts of the patriarchy, designed to hold women responsible for controlling the sexual urges of men. Stringent Sabbath practice is viewed as unnecessarily restrictive (and even anti-capitalist, which, in fact, it is). A strain of anti-religious (at least anti-Christian, anti-Jewish, and anti-Muslim) sentiment runs through the progressive world. Some tend to get misty-eyed when hearing about the work of organizations like Footsteps (which helps people "escape" their communities in Orthodox Brooklyn), with no such appreciation for stories of people converting *to* Orthodoxy. Maybe it's not quite believable that someone would voluntarily choose to live a more rule-bound life.

Seen through this lens, for a person to allow their religious commitments to limit their freedom is, prima facie, suspect; for such religious commitments to limit *other* people's freedom is unacceptable. More choice is imagined to be always preferable to less choice. And so in the name of equality, the supposedly neutral public square maximizes choice. This means formally accommodating everybody all the time (allowing everyone to swim during all hours), even if doing so effectively excludes a religious community from a public resource entirely.

If public facilities and services (schools and pools) are hypersensitive about making concessions for religious practices, this phenomenon plays out a hundredfold when money is involved. Native American claims on land or rivers or burial grounds as sacred territory do not stand a chance when a fossil fuel pipeline or other large corporate venture is at stake. (A significant exception to this rule was the Dakota Access pipeline, whose construction was halted in 2016 through an outpouring of public protest in which people asserted, along with the Standing Rock Sioux Tribe, that "water is life.")

Undue Hardship

Corporate employers are legally bound to make only limited allowances for the religious observances of their employees. Title VII of the 1964 Civil Rights Act required employers to accommodate their employees' religious practices—in theory. But the language was vague, and Congress later added a caveat: the employer has to make reasonable accommodations *unless* this would impose an "undue hardship" on the company.

What constituted undue hardship? The answer came in the 1977 Supreme Court case *TWA v. Hardison*. In this case, the plaintiff, Larry Hardison, argued that TWA (the airline) had violated his rights as a member of the Church of God in denying him his Sabbath as a day off from work. The Supreme Court ruled in favor of TWA, agreeing with its lawyers that to accommodate this employee's Sabbath would have imposed a greater than "de minimis" cost, meaning more than trivial or insignificant. That was all it took. More than trivial was deemed unreasonable.

This decision has since been revised by the Supreme Court in *Groff v. DeJoy* (2023), which was also a case about Sabbath accommodations. Here the court unanimously decided that an employer must accommodate the religious practice unless doing so would result in "substantial increased cost." While this is an improvement over de minimis cost, the default assumption is still that corporate profits take priority. Presumably the same vague metric applies to other religious practices—granting breaks for midday prayers or religious exemptions from a company's dress code or grooming rules. American jurisprudence fundamentally prioritizes corporate profit margins over religious practice.

The message is clear: If you want to participate fully in American social life—and earn the political capital that comes with that—you have to be willing to relinquish some of your religious life. Sabbath practice is optional, debate competitions are optional, modesty is optional, swimming is optional. People are expected to simply make their trade-offs and get on with their lives. The public need not make any sacrifices for the sake of religious communities; an employer need not bear any real cost to support the religious life of the employee. Wispy matters of the spirit are all well and good as long as they remain immaterial.

The Invention of "Religion"

As religious children, parents, workers, and would-be swimmers have been forced to make these hard choices individually, the cumulative change in American society has been clear: Religious life has been on the decline for decades; people are increasingly religiously unaffiliated and uneducated. More of us every day find ourselves in positions like David's (who wanted to bury his wife's body, but didn't), where we do not have the spiritual inner resources to grapple with life's big losses and questions, and we lack a sense of larger purpose. We don't fully understand what's at stake in the adoption of secular norms, nor do we have the language to challenge those norms if we do. We default to the thin consolations offered by the secular world and are left with an unplaceable sense of grief.

It has long been theorized that today's increase in depression, addiction, and suicide can be traced to the decline of religious engagement and community—coupled with the ubiquity of smartphones and screens that leave us isolated and disembodied. Statistically the connection is hard to prove, but anecdotally it seems to be true, and on a gut level it is blazingly obvious.

How did this happen? Where did it start? And could anyone have foreseen where it would lead us? We could trace the decline of religious life in the United States back to the European Enlightenment or the Protestant Reformation or even earlier. Countless factors, including economic and political ones, play into the history of the cleaving of "religion" from "regular life" and the subsequent waning of "religion." But before medieval times and certainly back in biblical times, there was arguably no such thing as "religion." "Religion" is a secular invention.

I was introduced to this concept in reading Talal Asad's classic *Genealogies of Religion* in graduate school (Asad is a scholar of Islam, Christianity, and religious studies generally). The very attempt to define "religion" as its own category with its own distinct essence is an artifact of modernity and of Christianity. Asad writes:

> It may be a happy accident that this effort of defining religion converges with the liberal demand in our time that it be kept quite separate from politics, law, and science.... This definition is at once part of a strategy (for secular liberals) of the confinement, and (for liberal Christians) of the defense of religion. Yet this separation of religion from power is a modern Western norm, the product of a unique post-Reformation history. The attempt to understand Muslim traditions by insisting that in them religion and politics (two essences that modern

society tries to keep conceptually and practically apart) are coupled, must, in my view, lead to failure.

Why does Asad predict this failure? Because in Muslim traditions, he argues, the essences of "religion" and "politics" were not separate to begin with. The notion of "religion" came from the West. Muslim societies have been prescient in recognizing that the threat posed by modernity *begins* with the attempt to extract something called "Islam" from the complex web of attachments, identities, histories, texts, relationships, and practices that constitute their world. Islamic societies, with their rich intellectual tradition, have shown clarity and discipline in resisting the attempt to define and thereby confine "religion." They recognized that once this happens and something called "religion" is placed on equal footing with secular powers, the third framework will rear its head and the game will be lost.

The simple act of constructing ancient practices, like Muslim practices, as a "religion" can cause irreversible spiritual damage. It introduces the notion that one's formerly immersive culture, community, spirituality, and way of life is an object, separate from oneself, that can be chosen or unchosen. Once this is seen, it can't be unseen; there will always be at least a fragment of a self that will stand lonely and apart from what used to be its entire world. Just as from the standpoint of modernity fundamentalism can produce trauma, from a traditionalist standpoint modernity can produce trauma. And while these dynamics may be especially visible in Islamic societies, all religious societies have had a similar struggle: once your "religion" is named, boxed, and relativized, there's no going back.

For the purposes of my exploration here, I see "religion" as modernity's most diabolically ingenious brainchild. In the process of artificially defining and prying apart two realms—matter (politics, military, economics) and spirit (religion, values, emotion, imagination)—matter gets tagged as "real" and spirit as "not real." There's a clear hierarchy—money is what makes the world go round; superior strength, guns, or military force will always win; people will always act in their material self-interest. When we're tempted to think that people are motivated by intangible sentiments like love, faith, or values (especially in, say, electoral politics), we're told, no, "it's the economy, stupid." James Carville's epithet "stupid" is crucial here—there's a powerful element of this discourse that shames us for such childish naivete.

Wherever matters of the spirit appear to have real power, the scientific wing of modernity's mansion busily reduces them to material phenomena. (Cue Ebenezer Scrooge in Charles Dickens's *A Christmas Carol* crying to Marley's ghost, "You may be an undigested bit of beef, a blot of mustard, a crumb of cheese, a fragment of underdone potato. There's more of gravy than of grave about you, whatever you are!") Especially in modern psychology and neurology, everything from love (oxytocin) to spiritual visions (an increase in N, N-dimethyltryptamine levels in the pineal gland) has a materialist explanation. Emotional states are explainable through the brain. Religious rituals are reduced to their possible psychological benefits to the practitioner. To think that they actually conjure unseen animate forces in our world would be foolish.

This materialist ideology seems to be the inverse of the ideology that governs the virtual world—where the important substance of a "person" is expressed immaterially while the physical body is at best an adornment to the self and at worst an encumbrance. (People will pay real money—that could be used for food or shelter—to deck out their virtual avatars with designer clothes and handbags or purchase weapons for them to use in online games.) But the maintenance of separation is at the heart of both dynamics. This separation is the underlying framework of the secular gaze. And it is in this separation that a primal wound of modernity is inflicted.

Where Did All the Religious Flower Children Go?

Faith communities of all stripes around the world have, by now, had to grapple with modernity in one way or another. Each has dealt with this challenge (and opportunity) in different ways. Rabbi Benay Lappe provides a useful framework for thinking about the encounter with modernity in what she calls the "1-2-3 Crash" model. When we are immersed in any traditional system of thought and practice—what she calls the "master story"—and we encounter something that challenges or doesn't fit its worldview, she says, we experience a "crash"—an episode of deep distress, confusion, and cognitive dissonance. At such moments, one of three things inevitably happens:

1. We deny the crash, revert to the master story, and try to shore it up to prevent more threatening information from getting in.
2. We accept the crash, decide that our master story is rotten to the core, throw it out entirely, and write a new master story.
3. We accept the crash *and* keep the master story, using the crash to understand the master story, possibly revise it, and tell it differently and creatively.

My parents chose option 2—acceptance of the crash and complete rejection of the tradition. And they were not alone. According to legend, the ocean floor around Ellis Island is littered with sheitels (marital wigs), tefillin (phylacteries), and yarmulkes thrown overboard by arriving Eastern European Jewish immigrants. Many of them anglicized their names (contrary to popular belief, names were not usually intentionally changed by customs officials). To what extent these actions represented a declaration of freedom and to what extent they revealed the imperative to assimilate fast, we'll never know. But many never found their way back to Jewish tradition, and each successive generation grew more remote from it.

Others coming from Jewish, Muslim, and other religious traditions chose option 1—build a high wall and hold on to the old paradigm, that is, some version of traditionalism. These communities recognized that modernity posed a threat to cherished lifeways. The core ideology of modernity, revolving around individual rights, freedoms, and capacities, directly contradicts spiritual teachings revolving around surrender to something larger than ourselves. From the perspective of traditions that value sublimating the self to God's will, modern virtues must seem dangerously crass, selfish, isolating, and spiritually bankrupt. At the same time, anyone can see the seductive appeal of secular life. It's not hard to imagine how the whole modern project could be experienced as an existential threat—and how resistance could feel crucial.

In the resistance to modernity, I am not intending to lift up fundamentalist societies as an ideal. There are very real systems of oppression and violence that plague many such communities. Activists from the inside have been calling for greater freedom and equality of opportunity for years now, especially for women and gender and sexual minorities. But I suspect that the repressiveness of these communities is itself at least partly a trauma response. The threat of liberal ideology can cause so much fear, it spawns an overcorrection. Harsh, punitive, inflexible, and at times inhumane interpretations of a tradition can come to the fore in a desperate attempt to stop the momentum before everyone starts slipping down the greased slide of secularism. It's much easier, the reasoning goes, if you don't get on the greased slide to begin with. Don't even climb the ladder.

Some of today's ultra-orthodox Jewish communities have reasoned in exactly this way, asserting a narrow and rigid interpretation of Jewish tradition. In this hermeneutic practice, nothing is permitted; everything is either required or forbidden. Leaders impose seemingly ever-tightening restrictions, especially around modesty, marriage, and *kashrut* (dietary laws). In a benign example, the Orthodox Union recently ruled that Impossible Pork is not kosher because, although it contains no actual pork, the "pork" in the product's name might confuse observant Jews. More problematically, in the name of modesty some ultra-orthodox sects are working to remove images of women from public view altogether. This is the danger inherent in Rabbi Lappe's option 1— the reactionary clinging to tradition. From a modern viewpoint it is an unconscionable social erasure. But it is also clearly an overplayed response to a fear of further spiritual slippage: at the bottom of this particular slippery slide is the toxic hyper-sexualization of women and girls in American culture.

Predictably, this traditionalist backlash against modernity has generated a popular counter-backlash: organizations like Footsteps are raising millions of dollars, Netflix originals like *Unorthodox* and *My Unorthodox Life* are flourishing, and masses of young people are fleeing religion altogether. Maybe the jettisoning of tefillin into New York Harbor was a progenitor of these backlash movements.

Although there are many principled reasons for people to reject parochial orthodoxies, I can't help but note also, coincidentally, how bad such orthodoxies are for corporate capitalism. It does the American economy no good for communities to spend much of the day engaged in non-monetizable activities (like group prayer), to revere media that was produced hundreds or even thousands of years ago (with little opportunity for sequels, merchandizing, or co-branding), to designate one day out of seven for intentional nonproductivity and nonconsumption, and to generate little need for new goods or services. So while it is no surprise that progressive-minded people flee constrictive religious communities, it would also be no surprise if the consumer economy quietly cheered the increasing repressiveness of such communities and the consequent flight of future consumers. We flee religion straight into the arms of capitalism.

I see this dynamic as a rolling tragedy in our world. The dialectical ping-ponging between secular modernity and strict religious traditionalism squeezes out the possibility of a more spiritually alive, creatively traditional, embodied, compassionate, and ecologically grounded religious adventure. (This would be roughly Rabbi Lappe's option 3, accepting the crash *and* keeping the master story, yet using the crash to understand the master story, possibly revise it, and tell it differently and creatively.)

Religious Fundamentalism as a Trauma Response

The history of Hasidism is, to me, a deeply sad but textbook example of how this process plays out. The early Hasidim of the eighteenth century were the Jewish flower children of their day. You could find them frolicking in the woods of Eastern Europe communing with God. You could hear raucous singing, praying, and ecstatic dancing coming out of their little *shtiebels* (private prayer gathering spaces). While they followed the laws of Torah scrupulously, they also thumbed their noses at established synagogues. They were mystical travelers, seeking the childlike, visceral spiritual connection that they found absent in mainstream practice. We could say that they were early practitioners of Rabbi Lappe's option 3, renewing and reinfusing the tradition with meaning.

The founder of the Hasidic movement, known as the Baal Shem Tov, said, "Unless we believe that God renews creation every day, our prayers grow habitual and tedious." He was alluding to a beautiful section of the Jewish morning liturgy that says, "And in Your goodness, renewing, every day forever, the making of creation . . ." Each day, even each moment, the universe is being dynamically re-created. All observant Jews would recite these words daily, but the Hasidim wanted to actually touch that live wire of continual creation through their practice.

This kind of joyful, innocent connection with the holy—or even the active pursuit of it—can be deeply threatening to entrenched power structures. So a counter-movement emerged in Eastern Europe known as the Mitnagdim or "opponents." They were traditionalists who had harsh words for these longhairs for taking too many liberties and failing to adequately keep the commandments (though the Hasidim saw themselves as fully observant). The laws of the Mitnagdim became increasingly restrictive as they struggled to define and sustain what they saw as authentic practice. The two groups soon became polar opposite archetypes—the Mitnagdim as dour, spiritually tight-fisted rule-enforcers, the Hasidim as rebellious religious adventurers.

In the late eighteenth century, however, everything changed as the Hasidim and the Mitnagdim were confronted with an even greater mutual threat: the rise of the Haskalah, or Jewish Enlightenment. In the face of this new and powerful movement, the differences between the two traditionalist groups suddenly seemed trivial. The polemic could no longer be sustained. In the bright glare of science and reason, both groups seemed antediluvian. The proponents of the Haskalah favored assimilation with the secular and Christian societies in which they lived, and I imagine that to them, the isolationist culture of the traditionalist movements was flat-out embarrassing. Capitalism reared its head in this story of secularization as well. The Haskalah had emerged concurrently with the spread of capitalism in Europe. It was carried on a wave of commerce and industry that had no patience for archaic religious concerns. To be too observant, to keep a Sabbath, or to be "too Jewish" was all bad for business.

By the time Hasidism and Mitnagdism reached American shores, they had mostly telescoped into each other. In Shaul Maggid's book, *American Post-Judaism*, he recounts a story in which the twentieth-century Hasidic leader Rabbi Joel Teitlebaum told his followers in Williamsburg, Brooklyn, that "Today there are no longer any Mitnagdim." Before they could get too excited about this news, he conceded that this was only because, "today there are no longer any Hasidim!" The flower children were nowhere to be found, and both movements had gotten subsumed into one struggling vestige of traditionalism on life support.

Looking at the practices of many Hasidic communities today, it seems that the creative, mystical tradition of Hasidism got distorted through this dynamic. The (sometimes well-earned) stereotype of the American Hasidic Jew today is one of joyless and rule-bound men wearing uncomfortable clothes and perpetually pregnant unhappy women, also wearing uncomfortable clothes. Whether true or not true or partially true, this is the public imprint of Hasidism today, and this is how far the movement has been pushed from its roots. It is *this* Hasidism from which Footsteps helps people escape.

In this story spanning hundreds of years, I see, writ large, the story of my family and so many other families in our day. An elderly relative of mine, Sam, grew up living with Orthodox grandparents who were the equivalent of the Mitnagdim for their era. In response to what I assume were hostile secular authorities back in the old country and to the spiritual threat of liberal Judaism, in America they doubled down on their traditional practices, hanging on by their fingernails to what they knew. Their lives (and therefore their children's and grandchildren's lives) were governed by endless rules, seemingly pointless and picayune. There were no reasons given for these rules and no connection to meaning or spirituality. From the accounts I've heard, it sounds like there was little joy in their family's religious life.

The children in Sam's family yearned for a life unstifled. It probably didn't help that the neighborhood non-Jewish kids whose lives *were* so unstifled would beat them up, assailing them as "Christ-killers." There was such pain wrapped up in some of the Jewish expressions of the twentieth century that people like Sam, at the earliest opportunity, fled as quickly and completely as they could.

Other Jews of that generation had experiences more like my mother's, where the Judaism of their more secular family was not particularly painful, but dry and meaningless. The Jewish traditions they kept were like a phantom limb, still operating for reasons no one could quite remember—perhaps just nostalgia. Many of the Jews at the UU churches where I served are in this category. The Judaism of their childhood wasn't terrible, but it wasn't compelling either. Antisemitism also operated among these more assimilated Jews. My mother grew up in a house next to a golf course where Jews were not allowed. And she believes to this day that she lost the love of her life because he and his parents couldn't stomach the idea of him marrying a Jewish woman. Ethnic particularity was detestable to mainstream American society—it was clear that full assimilation to the vanishing point was the cost of admission.

There was no option 3—adaptation and reinvention—for the vast majority of this generation of Jews. Experimentation certainly was happening on the fringes with creative reinterpretations of the tradition and joyful worship pioneered by "neo-Hasidic" spiritual teachers like Rabbi Zalman Shachter-Shalomi and Abraham Joshua Heschel. The Jewish Renewal movement as a whole is an embrace of this ethic of adaptation and reinvention. But in my experience, most Jews to this day have never heard of Jewish Renewal. And some Orthodox Jews consider Renewal Jews to be barely Jews at all. And as all of this nets out, the strategy of keeping the community together through stricter and stricter observance has backfired. It has brought about the very flight from the community that it was designed to prevent. Contrary to how it looks to progressive eyes, doubling down on tradition with harsh, legalistic exactitude bespeaks not power but powerlessness.

The dearth of options aside from either a harsh, doubled-down traditionalism or a complete abandonment of religious life has left many of us adrift today. We naturally yearn to find our people—our *am*—but every road we try feels like a dead end. Rabbi Benay Lappe's own story is a case in point. As she tells it in her TEDx Talk, "1-2-3 Crash," she was raised in a conservative Jewish family in Chicago, and her crash came when she was an adolescent and she suspected that she might be gay. She says that her first response was an option 1 response: deny it. She denied what she was feeling and who she was, even to herself. She tried to code herself as traditionally feminine, not wearing clothes that she liked because they looked too "masculine."

Then, for the first time, Lappe fell in love with a woman. The experience changed her, and she ran full speed to option 2 (abandoning the master story altogether). She left the Jewish world and became a Buddhist; she immersed herself in the lesbian community; she moved to Japan. She says, "I tried to get as far from my Master Story as I could." Initially, it was great. She recalls, "I had a fabulous time! Fabulous! That's the upside of Option #2. You don't have to deal with a Master Story that doesn't quite fit. You are free now. You are *loving* your new Master Story. I was happy, happy ... for a while." She reminds us that every master story eventually crashes. And this one did too. She realized that in leaving her original world to find her "real self," she had given up another big part of herself. And that was real too. She had lost the nourishing, connected parts of her traditions and family life—the *am*. And she had lost an ancient technology for spiritual connection. She said, "When you completely reject your Master Story, you also get rid of all the good stuff; the stuff that *was* true. And you let go of parts of yourself that you realize later were just not negotiable." It took her years to find her way back home.

Loss of Intimacy

Paul remembers the moment in high school when he decided to check his Facebook feed twice a day instead of just once. He laughs at this memory because now he checks Facebook or other social media accounts about every five minutes. Paul is a young man living in New York City, the adult son of an acquaintance of mine. He says Facebook has become automatic. Looking down at the phone screen has become as habitual as breathing. As much as Paul acknowledges this matter-of-factly, he's also disturbed by it. He gets headaches; he doesn't like the physical experience. And most of the time, he says, scrolling social media makes him feel bad.

He first noticed the diminishing returns around 2016 when it seemed that political discourse online was becoming more toxic. He saw that his social media friends' posts were more often shares of political content and less often "life updates." And to the extent that they did post life updates, this was often the only connection he had with them. He rarely felt moved to post his own updates. So the friendships felt one-way and, in his word, "artificial."

To address these issues with Facebook, first Paul tried tweaking the settings so that he would see more of what he wanted and less of what he didn't want. That didn't work.

Then he tried simply deciding to use Facebook less, but that didn't work either. Finally, he deleted the app from his phone, thinking that the awkwardness and inconvenience of using the web-based version would deter him. It didn't. He found himself logging on to the Facebook website and continued to use it, clunky as it was. Eventually he gave up and reinstalled the app.

TikTok was even more insidious. When you open the TikTok app, he points out, the video takes up whole screen. If you don't like the first video, you swipe, and it gives you something else. He found the algorithm to be incredibly sensitive and responsive. Within his first hour of using it, TikTok was serving him exactly what he likes to watch. "Serving" is an odd term here, of course, because in fact it is the users of these free services who are serving the company with their monetized attention and personal data. Google's former design ethicist, Tristan Harris, put it succinctly in the documentary *The Social Dilemma* when he said, "If you're not paying for the product, you are the product."

Paul tried to break free several times. He would put his phone down and get himself set up with some music and a good book to read. But a notification chime would suck him back in to watch a video. Finally he deleted the TikTok app, just as he had tried with Facebook. He sought out the same kind of videos on other platforms. But their algorithms were not as adept at delivering what he wanted, and so what he identifies as the "dopamine hit" was not as good. He reinstalled TikTok. Paul says, "It's the one that I think is most dangerous." After each video ended, Paul would tell himself, "just one more, just one more." He would keep watching one after another, and time would disappear. He says he once lost five hours this way.

Imagine a technology powerful enough to make time itself disappear. Of course, "losing five hours" is only a figure of speech, but this is the way that Paul experienced it. And what is time but our experience of moving through our lives on this earth? If Paul had little agency, derived no benefit, and perhaps doesn't even remember much of those five hours, they were indeed lost. A small but precious chunk of his brief life has been taken from him with only partial consent. Yes, it was he who kept swiping—there was no physical gun to his head. And yet, today's technologies create a gray zone where choice and agency start to break down. Social media is addictive by design.

Paul is now engaged with a screen almost constantly, either his work computer, his cellphone, or his TV. Often he is on two screens at once—a TV on in the background while working; on a work call on the computer while playing a mindless game on the phone. Paul considers his social media use an addiction. But it's not only its addictive qualities that keep him coming back. It is so deeply embedded in his being and his social world that he can no longer imagine life without it. It has changed the way he relates to the world. Crucially, it allows him to avoid embodied relationships while maintaining distant relationships.

On one hand, to be absorbed in his screens serves an escapist outlet from his strained relationship with his boyfriend. They can be physically in the same apartment together, but Paul's sense of self is powerfully engaged elsewhere. On the other hand, through social media he stays connected with "peripheral people" from whom he would otherwise drift away. It feels important to know at least the general contours of their lives, even if he never talks with them in person. More than once, he has found out about the death of a Facebook friend only because of the "RIP" messages of mutual friends. He was never close enough to the deceased that their family would have reached out to him directly. But it mattered to him tremendously to receive this important news. If only for this, he says, he could never give up social media. It's vital. "How else would I find out that friends are dead?"

Karat: To Be Cut Off from the People

I'm struck by a parallel between Paul's online death notification story and that of another young New Yorker, Jennifer, who similarly struggled to use her phone less but found it to be indispensable. Jennifer is the mother of a toddler, and she has been keenly aware of the need to carve out a private space for independence from her omnipresent phone, for her son's sake and for her own. So Jennifer started to experiment. She would take a few hours here and there, turning off her phone, and going out by herself to a beautiful place. Once there, she would take photos—a creative outlet she used to love but that fell by the wayside as online life filled more of her consciousness. She enjoyed these private, anonymous hours but also struggled with a sense of fear of missing out ("FOMO"), wondering what was going on in her absence.

On May 24, 2022, after one of these outings, Jennifer turned her phone on and discovered that while she had been offline the mass shooting of schoolchildren in Uvalde, Texas, had taken place. She felt bereft, scrolling through her feeds teaming with conversation threads, media analyses, crying emojis, and angry text reactions from her friends, all of which had been going on for hours without her. This validated her FOMO—she *had* in fact missed out on something important. It made her reluctant to turn off her phone again. In retrospect it had been painful. She had been disconnected, cut off.

In the Torah tradition, *karat*—to be cut off from the people—is a metaphysical punishment worse than death. It is reserved for only the worst sins. It deprives the sinner of the fulfillment of a primal human need—the need to stay continually connected to our people—our *am*—whoever they may be. We seek emotional, intellectual, and physical contact. We have evolved to crave this social connection—for protection, for getting food, and for love and sex. For most of our history, it has been dangerous to wander alone outside the tribe, dangerous to not be privy to up-to-date information about where the wild animals might be lurking or which plants might be safe to eat or who might be ready for marriage. To be cast out into the wilderness is a nightmare. The threat of *karat* is a gun to one's head.

Today's online communities function as our tribes. Through them we learn of dangers and opportunities, and certainly of food, love, and sex. These tribes are larger than the tribes and local communities of old, whose size was circumscribed by place and time. The online tribes' unlimited expansion has been made possible only by lifting off from the physical plane altogether. Despite all its current nastiness, this virtual space has become "civilization," (in contrast to the physical world, which has become "the wilderness"). It has become the nerve center of our society. And we need society no less urgently than ever. Given this, as Jennifer describes the experience, every hour without her phone is an hour of *karat*.

Technology as a Tourniquet

I am awed by all of the implications of Paul's and Jennifer's stories, especially realizing how common such stories are. What does it mean that one would learn of the death of a distant friend indirectly, through a screen, and that this would result not in remorse over the lack of intimacy with that friend but in greater loyalty to the technology that conveyed this data—or that one would experience *karat* when spending a few hours in the physical world and missing the news of a faraway tragedy? It's hard to believe that internet-based information would be accepted as a substitute for physical and emotional human contact. And yet it seems that for Paul, Jennifer, and many of us these days, life mediated through the internet is not only acceptable but essential.

If we trace it backward through time, what conditions need to be in place, what kind of world do we need to live in for this reality to have become possible? What could possibly make online living preferable to the alterative? A few things come to mind: First, we need to be physically dispersed, with friends far-flung around the globe. Career, personal ambitions, and economic necessities must have separated our families. Second, place and land must be ancillary to our sense of home. We must be alienated from *adamah* so that geography is seen as just an annoying technical barrier to be overcome. Third, the meaning of "friendship" must have blurred. It must now encompass a wide range of relationships, including that of the barest acquaintance (some online "friends" have never, in fact, met). Fourth, we need to live in a society in which we are so continually barraged with information about suffering and loss, near and far, that we could not possibly be obligated to do anything about any one instance of it. A cultural ethic must emerge in which we all act as life voyeurs commenting from the sidelines. It's all a reality show.

Add to all of this the experience of being buffeted by a politically divided and embittered society. Collectively we play and replay variations on the themes of racial and gender trauma. Our social problems feel intractable. The economic structures that feed our ecological crises are embedded in every facet of life. Corporate capitalism has reduced us to producers and consumers, monetizing everything that could give meaning to our lives, sucking us dry. If this is the real-world alternative to the virtual world, can you blame anyone for wanting to escape?

A case in point: My friend Vanessa, a Black woman in her sixties, explained that she greatly appreciates being able to shop online. It has been liberating for her to be able to avoid the casual, pervasive racism that she experiences in retail stores. When shopping in brick-and-mortar settings, she is followed and watched. She often feels the store workers' mistrust. They will sometimes express surprise when she buys an expensive item, assuming that because she is Black, she is poor. She explains that even when hailing a taxi, the driver is more likely to pick her up when she is with me, a white woman, than when she is alone. After centuries of struggle having failed to move the needle, she has little reason to believe that this will ever change—and certainly not in her lifetime. Online at least she is treated impartially. (This is not to say that she is finally treated like a human being online—none of us is. But she will take what she can get.) For Vanessa, and probably for many people of color in the United States, it is a relief to be able to shop in a space without bodies, where skin color is invisible.

All of this together is a heartbreaking snapshot of a broken world. And it reveals us humans as a foundering species, lost and alienated from our own bodies, from one another, and from the land. As for any mammal who might find itself in this predicament, it feels like our life force is draining out of us. And this is not just individual loss; the body of our collective *nefesh* is failing. The term *nefesh* expresses the dense vitality of the soul and the holiness of the body together. Just as we each are a *nefesh* individually, we all participate in the *nefesh* of our spiritual–physical communities and spiritual–physical planet. Each individual who experiences fragmentation experiences part of the wider fragmentation of our world. We are alienated from one another in a way that cannot help but be systemic, as an injury that affects the whole body.

And so our corporate internet-based technologies, which aggravated the injury, have now swooped in for a dramatic, improbable, and lucrative rescue. They give us the means to connect with each other, just barely, thinly but credibly. They serve as a tourniquet. They stop the bleeding. They save the patient. But they do not heal the wound. Instead, they say the wound is too deep to heal, and they sacrifice the limb.

Is the wound, in fact, too deep to heal? It certainly seems that most of us have reached that conclusion. Our embrace of the virtual world feels compensatory—we are giving up on the physical world. For good reason: If you look around, sometimes online living does seem better than the alternative. In the face of the failures and disappointments of modern life, it's understandable that we would want to cut our losses, avoid some pain where possible, and save what we can.

Covering the Mirrors

During a *shiva* (the seven days of Jewish mourning after the death of a loved one), the surviving relatives customarily cover over all the mirrors in the household. I just recently found out why. I had heard various explanations before, the most common one being that we cover the mirrors to avoid any concern for one's own appearance and focus entirely on the loved one who died. For this week, we are not presenting ourselves to the world or to the *shiva* guests; we are just allowing ourselves to mourn and to be held by the community. For some of us, this could be the first time we do not somehow truss ourselves up as an object for public consumption.

But my *mashpiah*, or Jewish spiritual director, shared an additional explanation for the covering of the mirrors—a more mystical one. She first explained that in the *kabbalah* (the received mystical tradition) a person is understood to have five levels of soul consciousness. The "highest," subtlest, and most ethereal is called *yechida*—our primordial essence, already unified with the divine light of God.

On the other end of the soul continuum is *nefesh*—the most earthly and physical. *Nefesh* is quite literally our soul-body. It's the whole person that we manifest in our daily lives. It's what we think of as ourselves. The soul and body aspects of our *nefesh* are inextricable from each other—inextricable, that is, until death. At the moment of death, the soul must for the first time disentangle itself from the body. The process of differentiation is believed to be wrenching, painful, and confusing for the soul. For the first few days the soul may fly, baffled, back and forth between the body in the grave and the *shiva* house where she lived her life. We cover the mirrors as an act of compassion for the visiting soul—to spare her the distress and fear of looking in the mirror and seeing no body. With patience and prayers, ultimately the soul lets go and returns to God.

To the modern mind, the idea of a soul being frightened by its own invisibility sounds superstitious and silly. Surely, we say, the idea of the soul is metaphorical at best. Even those who believe in the soul tend to see it as a more abstract entity—a sense of a self that continues beyond death, not some cartoonish ghost bereft over its lost body. And yet, as with so many folk and mystical teachings, this one taps into a deep truth of what we are as humans. The week after one's death may or may not play out as it's described in this account of the *nefesh* and the mirrors, but the idea that the rending of soul from body brings pain is entirely credible. Beyond credible, I believe that this painful rending is happening repeatedly in our world today, for most of us long before its natural arrival at the time of death. Our culture cleaves our souls from our bodies in a thousand ways, most vividly in our hybrid virtual/in-person existence. Our sense of self gets decorporated. And we suffer because of it.

The concept of *nefesh* has always been a powerful one to me. It feels deeply true: that what I think of as my "self" is both material and immaterial, and that the two dimensions are inseparable, at least for the purposes of this life on earth.

In chemistry terms, soul and body are a solution, not a mixture, within us. When I die and my body disintegrates, part of *me* will be diffused into the earth. I reject metaphors of the soul riding around in the body like it's some all-terrain vehicle, or of the body as "clothing" for the soul. Such metaphors denigrate the body while at the same time excusing the soul from any real engagement or investment in this world.

The Hugging Saint

Many ancient cultures have realized the integrated spiritual–physical essence of the human being and have developed practices and technologies for clearing away obstacles and promoting the divine flow through that being. Kundalini and other forms of yoga are sophisticated technologies for releasing the flow of bodily spiritual energy. Lagging thousands of years behind, as guru and yogi Swami Saraswati says, scientists are "discovering" the power of the body (in the same way that Columbus "discovered" America). Pop yoga and alternative medicine practitioners are also newly enthused about what they call the "mind–body connection." Bessel van der Kolk's best-seller, *The Body Keeps the Score*, became an international sensation as it powerfully articulated how our bodies store (and can release) trauma.

The technologies developed by the ancients suggest not separation but integration. In addition to yoga, these technologies include tai chi, qi gong, and other martial and training arts; Muslim *salat* prayers, which entail standing, bowing, prostration, and sitting; the practices of kneeling and of praying with rosary beads in Catholicism; the physical choreography of the Jewish liturgy; ecstatic dance in

Sufism and Hasidism; Chinese medicine; and the Indian medical science called Ayurveda.

In one unique case, the technology for plugging into the divine flow includes hugs. The living guru known as Amma is believed to embody divine maternal love, and she transmits it to those who visit her by hugging them. She's called "the Hugging Saint." Every summer she travels from her home in India to the United States to hug Americans, for free, by the tens of thousands. She fills convention centers for days on end with people lining up to receive one of her famous hugs. She has hugged more than 40 million people, often hugging thousands in a single day, one after another, from morning to evening, seemingly tirelessly. Some people sob in her arms while she rocks them; some leave radiant.

I have gone to see Amma several times, and while I have not experienced the hug itself as transformative, I have always felt an energy in the room that is unmistakably different from that of the world outside. There, in a sterile convention center, even waiting hours for my audience with her, it always feels joyful and peaceful. A band set up on the floor in front of her leads beautiful chanting; the food made by the chefs in Amma's entourage is delicious. The air feels lighter than it feels elsewhere. This spiritually elevated place has, at its heart, a flesh-and-blood person physically connecting with others.

Amma was hugging people long before the advent of Meta, X, TikTok, and hug emojis, and she certainly didn't start it to make a political or cultural point. But today, set against the backdrop of a society sliced through with screens, her simple act of touch becomes a rebuke. It proclaims that human touch, when expressing love, is holy and irreplaceable. If we're being honest, there is nothing that has ever transpired on a computer screen or in a virtual reality arena that has ever even approximated the experience of a loving hug (not to mention sex, massage, or other more intense forms of touch). It's fitting that the hug emoji itself looks so awkward—a yellow smiley face with two hands reaching out from where its jaws should be. The graphic designers must have been stymied—how to represent a hug with just a head and no body; just one being, not two; and in two dimensions, not three. Despite their earnest efforts, they couldn't do it.

Some might counter, well of course a hug emoji can't replicate a hug! It's not supposed to. It's just a symbol of hug. Symbolic representation is the best we've had so far. The reason the online world feels so woefully inferior to the physical world is that our technology is simply not yet sophisticated enough for more. It's not yet an adequate simulation of the sensory experiences of real life. But someday it will be, argue the proponents of virtual reality. It's already getting there. It will plug directly into our brains. It will be just like the physical world, just as real, but better.

Tech-Fueled Disembodiment: The Bifurcated Life

The emoji in general—often a disembodied head—is the perfect symbol for our new, strange era in which the mind, soul, or self is seen as separate from the body. We participate in the gleaming world of the emoji at the expense of our *nefesh*: Our bodies wind up in one place doing one thing while our sense of self winds up "elsewhere." We use the language of travel and experience to describe our online adventures, saying that we "go places" and "do things," forgetting that in truth we are sitting in one place and doing very little. Typically, in the words of one Facebook user, what we are actually doing is "sitting in front of a bright picture frame and touching buttons on a tray in a special sequence."

We spend greater and greater portions of our lives in this bifurcated state. Our bodies sit in the physical world, and what we increasingly think of as our "self" dwells in a virtual world. Worldwide internet users now spend a daily average of two and a half hours using social media. (Facebook, for one, has roughly three billion users. That's almost half the population of the entire world.) And most of us in the professional class use our computers and phones for an additional eight to twelve hours daily. Whether we work remotely or in person at an office, much of that time is spent communicating with people who are not in the room with us.

As recently as a hundred years ago, this would have been almost impossible; at that time the landline telephone was just starting to come into general use. If you wanted to communicate, you had to either be in the room with someone or write a letter. For that matter, you couldn't listen to music without being in the presence of a musician. You couldn't hear a story without sitting with a storyteller. You couldn't watch dance without being near dancers or drama without being around actors. A hundred years ago, humans still lived our lives primarily in the physical world, in our bodies, interacting with the bodies of people, other animals, and plants. Even those who subscribed to a religious or philosophical belief in the separation of spirit and flesh lived day-to-day lives as integrated beings. Now for many of us, especially in wealthier societies, that is no longer the case.

In today's bifurcated time, something precious is lost: The rich three-dimensional world is flattened into two dimensions. We withdraw to our separate cells. We continue to interact with each other through Zoom and other online media, but it is without smell or touch. When I meet with a friend via Zoom, we cannot make eye contact. His image is interpreted by the video camera on his computer and then again by the screen on mine. We cannot sing together. The sound waves of his voice are captured by his microphone and then approximated, with lag time, through my computer speaker. I control exactly what he sees of me and my surroundings (I can check my image on the screen before I click to join the call), and he controls what I see of him. Either one of us can end the call and disappear in an instant.

The value of what is now called meeting "IRL," in real life, is ineffable, hard to define or measure. But from what I have experienced and seen, the loss of it brings profound grief. We don't have a language for this kind of grief. We can't quite put our finger on it. So we often name it something like "Zoom fatigue"—the feeling of malaise, familiar to many of us, from spending too many hours on Zoom. A scientific account for this fatigue has to do with our brains having to work hard to continually reconcile audio and video that are not perfectly synced. And of course there's the eye strain from staring at a screen for hours on end, carpal tunnel from repetitive use of the keyboard, and back problems from bad posture at our computers. For each of these problems, there is a scientific explanation and often the promise of a technological fix. But as with so many purely materialist explanations, this approach misses a layer.

It misses the profound unnaturalness of the whole enterprise. Like a circus bear forced to balance on a ball, we humans are being made to repeatedly perform for our livelihood an act that denies our nature. I can feel, quite literally in my bones, that I was not made to be sedentary all day, using only my brain to direct abstracted versions of work and play through a rectangular panel. It's not what my animal body wants. My eyes glaze over; my shoulders sag under the strange weight of this weightless life. I feel my libido draining from me—libido in the larger sense of psychic drive or energy. I was not made for this. I was made to be fully engaged in this life in all dimensions of my being, working side by side with the people of my community, caring for others with my hands, breathing the outdoor air and gazing at the horizon. The loss of this natural human engagement is painful for me, and I sense that it is for many of us.

If we listen carefully, we can almost hear the rending of the *nefesh* over and over—the body on a couch in New York City, the self in an online game, perhaps a Fortnite "battle royale" on a lush virtual island; the body in an Indiana suburban basement, the self at a remote appointment with a doctor at the Medical Center five miles away; the body in a dark kitchen at 9 p.m. in Mill Valley, California, the self on a Zoom meeting on a sunny morning in Bangalore, India. Just as in the week after death, in the panicked alienation between body and place, place and self, self and body, I imagine the soul rushing back and forth in distress, searching for a natural home that no longer exists. We did not necessarily ask for this bifurcated life, but it has happened anyway, first slowly and then quickly.

Contactless

In the United States, we have long embraced individualism as an ideal. As political, economic, and psychological subjects, the maintenance of "healthy boundaries" with others is considered a marker of maturity and success. Since COVID-19, "healthy boundaries" have taken on a double entendre—the term connotes psychological health in the sense of protecting one's private space, consent-based romance, the right to stay within one's comfort zone, and physical health through the potentially life-saving practice of social distancing.

In the process, our interconnectedness with our *am* and with the other creatures of the earth, is a pleasant idea but not something urgent and real or religious. It is not something that guides our lives in any real way. Our lives are much more guided by the need to safeguard our own interests and those of our family. Others are let into that circle cautiously on a case-by-case basis. You can't really blame us for this. We have a paltry safety net, so in some sense it really is everyone for themself. And in this country, we have the historical anomaly of single-family homes and single-driver cars. More than a quarter of us live alone. As a measure of how little we trust each other, almost half of us live in homes with a gun.

And then, tossed like a grenade into the middle of this polarized society, is the centrifugal force of technology. As much as it connects us, it also pushes us away from each other. Any spare moment when we might have chatted with strangers—in line at the grocery store, in an elevator, in a waiting room—we're on our phones instead. Food delivery apps and online shopping make it less likely that we're going out in public to begin with. Trucks delivering "contactless" e-commerce goods by the hundreds of thousands of units per day congest our highways and city streets. And when we do have to share space with another human being, like in an Uber, the app now gives us the option of warning the driver in advance to not talk to us.

Naomi Klein's book *The Shock Doctrine* helps explain what's happening. In the process of what she calls "disaster capitalism," neoliberal free market forces leverage moments of crisis. As in New Orleans after Hurricane Katrina, when everyone is distracted, disoriented, and desperate for solutions, they quickly institute policies and programs that will solve the short-term problem while also institutionalizing greater concentration of power and wealth. The COVID-19 pandemic has been a disaster like Hurricane Katrina but with global reach.

The most obvious winners in the COVID-19 disaster capitalism game are the videoconferencing, social media, and streaming platforms whose user base has gone through the roof. But the crisis has also been a windfall for online retail. Since online shopping became available in the 1990s, it went from being a mode of novelty to one of convenience to one of safety (during COVID-19) to one of necessity today. Amazon reported a 200 percent increase in profits during the pandemic.

Around the world, hundreds of millions of people pay a monthly tribute of $14.99 for unlimited next-day delivery with Amazon Prime. This tribute represents both an acknowledgement and an investment in a life organized around online purchasing as well as streaming entertainment with Prime Video. My brother and sister-in-law, like many people (especially those in personal crises like illnesses or new parenthood) readily confess that they could not live without those next-day Amazon deliveries. The government agrees. If you qualify for government assistance, you can now get Amazon Prime for $6.99 per month. Everybody needs it. In this way the shock doctrine plays out at the individual level as well as the societal level.

Using the shock doctrine, disaster gets leveraged most effectively by the Amazons of the world—the giant, multinational, faceless corporations. As we buy more and more online, small businesses fail, never to return. Small businesses that employ and serve people in a local community, and in fact play a role in creating community, get steamrolled. As local businesses disappear, embodied relationships disappear with them. We no longer know the kindly pharmacist who will let us know when it's time to reorder a medication. Our kids are not invited to come work at the corner store as soon as they're of age. We can no longer joke around and make bad puns with the grocer—because the pharmacy, the grocery, and the corner store are gone.

On a much deeper psychospiritual level, then, it's corporate and moneyed interests writ large that have hit the jackpot. We've become a society of passive consumers sitting at home, forever trying to scratch an itch that can't be scratched through a screen. People sometimes complain about the closing of "mom and pop" stores. Some miss the in-person shopping experience (while for others it's good riddance). Some bewail the loss of consumer power as monopolies grow across all industries. Some mourn the hollowing out of local communities. Some even bristle at the physical experience of hours in front of screens trying in vain to replicate embodied experiences. But that hum of background grief over the loss of our embodied lives is not enough to compel change. In fact, from the perspective of disaster capitalism, it's good. Grief is a key propellant of the consumer society.

Hongi

Imagine these two scenes. Scene one, set in the North Island of New Zealand: A visitor from out of town comes to a Maori neighborhood and greets a shopkeeper. The two of them make eye contact and then lean their faces close until their foreheads and noses are touching. They take a moment to breathe each other's air before stepping back. And then they chat. This is the traditional practice of *hongi*—a greeting that means roughly "the sharing of breath."

The Maori creation myth, like the biblical creation myth, features the divine breathing life into an earth creature. The earthling becomes animated and conscious when it receives that breath of life. So in the practice of *hongi*, it's understood that the two people are literally sharing the breath of life, allowing it to pass between them. They are breathing life into each other. For a visitor, *hongi* is also a kind of initiation—they are being brought into the circle of the community, which includes all the creatures of the island and the *adamah* herself. They are taking part in the oneness of everything.

Scene two, set on the R train in New York City: A visitor from out of town gets onto the subway. He looks around, and seeing that every single person is on their phone, he gets out his phone too. He spends his ride in silence, transported through that little rectangular portal to a world that is not New York City but the world of Pokémon GO or Instagram or maybe an inflammatory news story. No one on the train acknowledges our visitor, and certainly no one has any interest in breathing his air. In fact, in the United States, we spent several years going to great lengths to avoid breathing each other's air.

In the age of COVID-19, *hongi* sounds terrifying. And in fact, during the height of the pandemic, Maori communities were trying to ban it or at least discourage it. But I want to suggest that in our culture *hongi* would have sounded terrifying even before COVID-19. We've been drifting away from each other for decades at least, and now some describe it as an "epidemic" of loneliness. Just as our culture was pushing us away from each other, increasingly mediating our interactions through screens, a disease came along that made it, for a time, positively reckless to be in the presence of another human being. I don't believe that this is coincidence but rather a prime example of the intertwining of the spiritual and material worlds. We experience the process of cultural alienation on many levels at once.

It seems that the Maori understand, perhaps more clearly than those of us in Western cultures, that there is a kind of physical and psychic vulnerability required to truly connect with others and experience the world. Intercourse between any two beings implies mutual porousness, which inevitably entails risk.

In studying the role of smell in Judaism, I was introduced to the wonderful concept in the field of olfaction: "volatility." The volatility of an object determines its smelliness. Here volatility means the quality of being in motion—actively morphing through contact with one's environment. The more porous the object, the more its edges are frayed, the more it continually sheds itself into the air or liquid around it, the smellier it is. If an object is static, with hard edges, boundaried and distinct from its environment, it has little smell. This is why a mammal's body is odiferous while a pane of glass is not. This is also why, while a homemade pizza can have wonderful aroma, the Instagram picture of that same pizza cannot.

Some version of this notion of volatility seems key for the other dimensions we perceive through the sensorium as well. All sensing is relational—the one being sensed has to give of itself, and the one perceiving has to receive into itself. Both are changed by the encounter.

For something to be *tasted*, it has to be partially dissolved if not destroyed (you can't enjoy the taste of a ripe blueberry without destroying it). For a sound to be *heard*, the sound waves first have to leave their source and then physically collide with the body of the listener. *Touch* between sentient beings transforms both as subtle energy currents travel between them, and they each shed and gain cells from the other. *Light* that bounces from one object to the eye of its observer forges a connection between them— so much so that according to the Heisenberg uncertainty principle an object is changed by being observed. And we know intuitively how a person can change by being observed. A "contactless" life may be safer in some ways, but it is a sterile and lonely life. Only by embracing volatility do we get the full relational juiciness of this world.

Teenage Stoners Playing Music in the Basement

As we humans spend more and more time online in a zero-volatility environment, we are starting to forgo even our evolutionary imperative to have sex and reproduce. The birthrate in Japan has been dropping dramatically, and in surveys and speculation, they're finding that—among other reasons—it's because people are scared of each other. They'd rather watch online porn or play games than risk face-to-face contact with all its uncertainty and vulnerability. Here in the United States, too, teenagers are going out with their friends less, dating less, getting more depressed and anxious, and having less sex—which has the happy side-effect of fewer teen pregnancies, but the reason is disturbing: we're effectively deciding that we'd rather spend time alone on our phones than have sex.

Sex aside, we have too little touch. With all the cases of violent and unwanted touch in the public awareness these days, we forget that touch is something that we need as physical *adamah*—beings. Babies and even monkeys who don't get touched can die. Elderly people with too little touch suffer much more from depression and disease. We humans need physical contact and eye contact with other human beings. And we're not getting it.

I remember vividly the distress with which a congregant, Joel, talked with me about his teenage daughter. He described a recent sunny Saturday when the family was planning to rent bicycles and go for a ride along the waterfront. The night before, his daughter had said she wanted to join, but when morning came, she was on her phone and no longer wanted to go. Her parents and brothers tried to entice her to come, to no avail. While her family enjoyed the day out exploring new parts of the city, she stayed in her room, in her bed, with the shades drawn, on her phone, all day. That particular Saturday was only one of many times Joel had tried to encourage her to do something in the real world. Her response was often, "I'm too tired." He said that she gets plenty of sleep and does not do physical labor or run marathons. She is exhausted by her sedentary life.

Joel explained that like most of her peers, she spends most of her free time on her phone. She goes nowhere without it, and but for the intervention of her parents, it would accompany her to bed at night. She uses it as late as she can—never voluntarily relinquishing it—and retrieves it first thing in the morning. Her social life is largely mediated by her phone. Although it is a "dumb phone" that can't access social media, she is constantly immersed in text conversations and group chats to the exclusion of the outside world. Even when she is with a friend in person, Joel observed, they often sit together texting other friends and showing each other things on their phones. She has never had a romantic relationship in person—only a long-distance relationship that took place entirely through text and the occasional phone call. That relationship had ended with the painful realization that the boyfriend had never really cared about her—but that she had been unable to read the signals via text.

Joel contrasted his daughter's experience with the memories of his own teenagerhood. As a middle-schooler, he was already playing in rock bands and semiregularly doing gigs at dances and older kids' proms. The kids rehearsed in their families' basements, often in a haze of marijuana smoke (this was the 1970s, after all). Their music-making was not mediated by anything or anyone; they were actually playing their instruments and bonding over the sounds that came from their guitars, microphones, drum kits, and amplifiers. It was a social enterprise of learning, sharing, and (often loudly) working out plans and disagreements. In this highly relational life, relationships with girls figured prominently. By the end of high school, Joel had had several romantic and sexual relationships, fallen in love, and had the classic human experience of getting his heart broken.

Physical activity permeated Joel's life. He ran on his school's track team and was frequently involved in pick-up games of baseball, employing a combination of the natural and built environments: a tree might be first base; a manhole cover could serve as home plate. The competition was loose, and the playing was the point. The telephone (landline of course) was useful only in so far as it facilitated working out the time and place for gathering. As he recalls it, when he was tired, it was that good, satisfied feeling of having played his heart out on the ball field or at the show.

Joel joked about the irony of wishing that his daughter had more sex, drugs, and rock 'n roll in her life, but that's exactly what he wishes. It pains him to see her living what he thinks of as a halfhearted half-life, missing so much of the vividness, excitement, and relational intensity of his own youth. She quite literally doesn't know what she's missing.

OCULUS™ Go

"Open your eyes. You are a fisherman in the Pacific, a weaver in the Philippines, and a journalist on the front lines. You act with kindness; you fight with courage. You swim the depths of the oceans; you float the heights of the skies. You walk on top of the world and you are someone else's world. You are with family; you are with friends; you are with ancestors."

So goes the voiceover for an ad for OCULUS Go, a virtual reality headset that allows you to virtually travel to all these places and be all these things. As the female voice narrates the virtual experiences you can have, the images are gorgeous. You see the fishermen in their wet yellow rain slickers hauling in baskets of shining fish; you see the earthy colors of the weaver's loom in the Philippines. When she says, "you're a journalist on the front lines," you see an urban stairwell shredded by shrapnel. When she says, "you are someone else's world," you see a baby staring up at you with wonder. And when she says, "you are with ancestors," you see a Native American drumming circle around a bonfire. The images flash faster and faster—all the choices, all the things you can be, all the experiences you can have without even having to get out of bed. You can order this thing on Amazon for $200, and if you have Prime, you'll get free shipping and have it by tomorrow. In the words of the ad, you can "live every story."

It's all immensely seductive. Where the physical world has limits, the virtual world is limitless. Where our own bodies can't do certain things, in the virtual world we can do anything. Where in real life the laws of time and space dictate where we can go, in the virtual world, we can go anywhere any time. Real fishermen *pay* for their experience of the ocean in sweat and injuries and backbreaking labor. With OCULUS Go, we get it for free. Real weavers in the Philippines pay for their immersion in the rich colors of the threads by decades of practice and monotonous, tedious work for dollars a day. We get it for free. Real parents pay for the wonder of their baby's love in sleepless nights and countless sacrifices. We, the wearers of the OCULUS Go headset, sacrifice nothing.

And it's all free from unpleasant political realities. A virtual Native American drummer isn't freighted with a history of genocide and oppression. A virtual beautiful woman is never going to turn to you and say, "No, thanks."

The OCULUS Go ad ends with this line: "Live every story. Because when you learn to love a life different from your own, the world becomes a little closer." That sounds so romantic, but the truth is, we cannot live every story. We are finite beings, and it's all we can do to fully live our *own* story. And if we really want the world to become a little closer, the real challenge is to bridge the enormous gulf between ourselves and our closest neighbor. To commit ourselves to that—to be present with who we actually are and to open ourselves to the physical presence of the other; to look into the eyes of another human being—that is as wild a ride and as much adventure as any of us can ever really handle.

Tech-Fueled Dislocation

The surreal screen-based universe of ones and zeros that we've created is, put simply, not real. When we deny this fundamental truth, we do so at great risk and great cost. And deny it we do. Virtuality is becoming not just play but a growing collective misunderstanding of what we are. With our virtual desktops, virtual navigation systems, virtual meetings, virtual gaming, virtual doctors, virtual communities, virtual assistants, virtual tours, and virtual shopping, we are creating an entire parallel reality—a life overlay. It's all easier than real life, and most of it is free or close to free. We forget that it's not real, and in our forgetting, it takes on a phantom reality of its own. We are godlike, re-creating the world but at one level removed.

Picture the American highway. If we use GPS to get around, we may never actually know where we are. Our knowledge of the *adamah*, the landmarks, and the progress of the sun across the sky—our internal global positioning system—fades as we cede ground to the "tech-xperts." We just follow the directions of the confident GPS voice—turn here, exit there, and arrive at your destination. It's like playing a video game. The highway stretches out infinitely in front of us. The road on the screen becomes more real than the road beneath our wheels. In an article for the *New York Times*, Greg Milner writes:

> Faith is a concept that often enters the accounts of GPS-induced mishaps. "It kept saying it would navigate us a road," said a Japanese tourist in Australia who, while attempting to reach North Stradbroke Island, drove into the Pacific Ocean. A man in West Yorkshire, England, who took his BMW off-road and nearly over a cliff, told authorities that his GPS "kept insisting the path was a road." In perhaps the most infamous incident, a woman in Belgium asked GPS to take her to a destination less than two hours away. Two days later, she turned up in Croatia.

When forced to choose between the map and the territory, we defer to the map. Our confidence in our own ability to see the land in front of us and trust what we're seeing fails.

My husband Jeff and I recently traveled by subway from Manhattan to Brooklyn to go to a friend's place for dinner. We got the address wrong and ended up far from where we were supposed to be. Since we were already running late at that point, we decided to call a Lyft to take us back the other direction to our friend's neighborhood. We typed the correct address into the Lyft app (or so we thought), and in a few minutes the Lyft arrived and we got in. There was no need to tell the driver where we were headed since he already had the address in the system. There was no need to talk to the driver at all except for a quick hello. Jeff and I were chatting, checking our email, and not paying much attention until suddenly we noticed that we were approaching the Williamsburg Bridge heading back toward Manhattan. Alarmed, we told the driver that we didn't want to go to Manhattan—the address was in Brooklyn. He insisted that, no, the address was in Manhattan. Jeff looked at his phone, and sure enough, we had not entered the word "Brooklyn," and so the address had defaulted to Manhattan.

What happened next could only have happened in today's strange, tech-distorted world. The driver informed us that if we wanted to change the destination, we would have to change it in the app. He couldn't take us to a new destination simply because that was where we now said we wanted to go. It had to be done through the system. So while we fiddled with the app, trying to figure out how to make the change, he continued over the Williamsburg Bridge and into Manhattan.

I do not fault the Lyft driver for this. He probably had no way to make a destination change in the system and limited ability to navigate New York City without the app. As we all increasingly rely on GPS for navigation, we start to lose the ability to relate directly to the urban or rural landscape around us. Or perhaps we never develop it to begin with. We surrender our own cognitive map of the real world and even sometimes our common sense. Even drivers become passive riders, putting our faith in this authoritative technology, guided by the satellites on high.

I can't help but think that if we had hailed an old-fashioned taxi, this story would probably have played out quite differently. We would have gotten in the cab, greeted the driver, and learned that his name was, say, Frank. We would have told him where we were headed. If he was unclear about whether we meant Brooklyn or Manhattan, he would have asked, and we would have clarified. And if, somehow, we still ended up heading in the wrong direction, or if we had changed our minds, we would have told him, and most likely Frank would have been capable of turning around and renavigating. Especially older cab drivers who learned to navigate the city without the benefit of GPS are often extraordinarily nimble, with a deep bank of geographical knowledge, an intuitive understanding of traffic patterns, and an ability to find even the most obscure locations. In this hypothetical scenario, the difference would have lain in a combination of engagement with the *am* (in the relational moment with the cab driver) and the driver's engagement with the *adamah* (his spatial understanding of the landscape).

Adamah versus Virtus

Everything on the ubiquitous screen has a kind of uniform sheen and sparkle—a commanding presence that makes us pay attention. Instagram stars get paid big bucks to convey a "lifestyle," and we take note. Even things that are in real life gritty and harsh, like the devastation from an earthquake, have a kind of romantic shine on a screen. Everything is clean, and even when it's made to look dirty, that dirt never really sticks. Stay online, and you never get dirty and you never get hurt.

And so virtuality represents a kind of collective dream—a world where everything is simple. It's two-dimensional, even when it creates the illusion of 3D. We've recreated reality but with latex gloves on. It's life abstracted. It lives on the plane of ideas and images and denies the earthly plane.

In some archetypal systems this cerebral, rational world is the masculine, whereas the embodied, emotional world is the feminine. This is not to say that women aren't rational; cosmic energies interplay, and women and men participate in both. But as a society, we are catapulting headlong into the world of the disembodied mind, which has long been linked with male prerogative, and we are collectively deciding that it's better than our voluptuous earth-bodies.

The etymology of the word "virtual" is helpful here. It comes from the Latin *virtus* ("virtue" in English) which meant "excellence, potency, efficacy." It also meant "manhood" or "manliness," from the Latin root *vir*, which means man. So "virtual" in the fourteenth century basically meant "good and manly." And down the line virtual came to mean what it means today. The virtual world is virtually the same as reality itself, only better and more manly. It's almost as if the virtual world is primary—like Plato's "forms"—the virtual is the ideal while the physical is just a pale imitation. It's as if virtuality is heaven to us.

So we have two worlds before us: the shiny, platonic, *virtus*-virtual world and the earthy, messy, *adamah*-physical world—the wetware, as they call it. We all know which is ascendant right now. Sears—which used to be the largest retailer in the United States—has closed its doors. It stands in a string of giant retailers (including Toys 'R' Us, Pier 1 Imports, and Modell's Sporting Goods) to do so. Little mom-and-pop shops are closing every minute as Amazon now sells online everything they used to sell but for less. We are in the midst of what experts are calling a "brick-and-mortar retail fiasco." Some speculate about whether brick-and-mortar stores will even exist ten or twenty years from now. Print publications are shutting down, one after another, as people get their corporate news and entertainment for free online. New York's *Village Voice*—an alternative newspaper—is a recent casualty. The iconic red plastic boxes are empty all over the city. The physical world is failing.

Runaway climate change and other ecological breakdowns shows us that the natural physical world is also failing. And I can't help but think there is a connection. We are embracing cerebral *virtus* and closing our eyes to Mother Earth. We are so entranced by the logic of virtuality we have forgotten how organic matter works. Our collective fantasy is crashing into our reality with devastating effects.

The stakes are high in playing God in this way. It misteaches us about the nature of reality. As we can draw and erase on a screen, change themes and colors at will, we've forgotten that the natural world is not malleable like that. As location is irrelevant in cyberspace and one's address is in "the cloud," we've forgotten that ecosystems are place-based and cannot be moved—each serves a vital, irreplaceable function on earth. As a click of a mouse creates instant effects, we forget that in the natural world, change takes decades or millennia—the global warming we're seeing today is because of fossil fuels burned years ago. As we can easily hit "delete" on a screen or move something to the trash and throw it away, we've forgotten that there is no "away"—there's only moving our waste from one place to another. As virtual space is infinite, we've forgotten that space on earth is finite. And as life online is largely free and easy, we've forgotten that anything worthwhile on earth takes effort, time, work, and even sacrifice.

Plato got it exactly backward: *This world* is where it's happening. This world is not a wanna-be imitation of some ideal world of forms in the clouds. Actually, it is the virtual world of "the cloud" that is an imitation of physical life on earth. God is at least as present in the *adamah* as in the *virtus*. In the physical world, and even in its limitations, we discover holiness. We can immerse ourselves in the unrepeatable beauty of a particular place and specific time, of seasons that change, of leaves that fall from trees, of things that fade and die. We can take a moment to marvel at our own skin, the miracle of our own volatile *adamah*-bodies, made of the bodies of everything and everyone who came before us. And we must reground in this world before it's too late.

Living in a Material World

As I started to learn about Jewish tradition, one of the qualities I first loved was its gritty materiality:

> Blessed are You, God, our God, sovereign of the universe, who formed the earthling with wisdom and created within him many openings and many hollows. It is obvious in the presence of your glorious throne that if one of them were ruptured, or if one of them were blocked, it would be impossible to exist and stand in your presence. Blessed are You, God, who heals all flesh and performs wonders.

So goes what is known as the Jewish "bathroom prayer"—the prayer recited after using the bathroom. It is found in most standard Jewish prayer books. In my home, this prayer is taped to the wall near the toilet. It may seem incongruous with what we normally think of as "spiritual" to evoke crude images of the workings of our sphincters. The concept of "spirituality" in Western societies tends to be inflected with a distrust of the body and its base, animalistic impulses. To get close to God, one is taught to reject the physical—through denial, abstinence from pleasures, and concealment—in favor of the spirit. The clerical robe that I used to wear on Sundays signals one part angelic, two parts academic, and zero parts physical. It conceals most of the body by design.

By contrast, Jewish prayer is earthy. The Torah is rarely ethereal, although angelic beings certainly make appearances in it and in liturgy. We are continually reminded that we are physical beings—mammals—whose existence is utterly dependent on the precise functioning of our bodies, as well as the supply of air we breathe, the food we eat, the earth we're made of, and the water we drink. In the Hebrew scriptures, God's blessings are mostly described in material terms—rain, fertility, abundant harvest, and safety from enemies. The penalty for sin is always expulsion from the land.

When God—or the wisdom-flow of the cosmos—created the world we know, biblical and evolutionary accounts agree that the stuff of creation was all rock and fire and water that became earth, which became our bodies. Quite pointedly, in Genesis we are called earthlings, creatures made of earth. We are physical beings, and everything that we are springs from the soil beneath our feet. We are literally what we eat. We are what we breathe. We are shaped by the billions of microorganisms who live in our guts. We are shaped by those whom we physically touch. We are living in a material world, and we are material beings.

In his classic work *Carnal Israel*, the Talmud scholar Daniel Boyarin writes passionately about the primacy of the body in Jewish tradition and rabbinic culture specifically. I first read this in a class on the Talmud, and it was thrilling. It confirmed—with academic heft—my intuitions about Jewish theology as a theology that celebrates our earthly lives as sacred. Although it was written over three decades ago about a culture that originated two millennia ago, the book reads as a bold critique of the disembodiment of our time. Boyarin traces the discourse of the early Christian fathers, like

St. Augustine, who charged the Jews with being "carnal," concerned with "the flesh," and literal in their interpretation of the commandments. "Augustine knew what he was talking about," writes Boyarin. "There was a difference between Jews and Christians that had to do with the body."

Boyarin explains that at least for Greek-speaking Christians, Hellenized Jews, and all who embraced Plato's theory of forms, "the essence of a human being is a soul housed in a body." Everything in the material world has a spiritual "signified," meaning that it is only important insofar as it symbolizes something in the ethereal world of ideas. The material world is profane and illusory; the spiritual world is sacred and real. With this view, Bible stories are allegorical, commandments are metaphorical, and carnal concerns (including marriage and sex) are distractions from the spiritual life, ideally to be minimized or avoided. (Modern Christians do not all, of course, embrace this view, but this was an early fork in the road, where the followers of Jesus split off from the theology of his Hebrew lineage.)

For rabbinic Jews, by contrast, the human being was understood to *be* a body, animated by a soul. Like a gadget animated by a battery, they belong together in this world. The gadget is the point; the battery on its own is useless. The body was important for its own sake, not as a vehicle or a metaphor for something else. The events of the Torah were real and historical, not allegorical. And the commandments were meant to be kept actually, not symbolically. The earth was a gift, and its abundance to be celebrated. Marital sex and procreation were seen as a positive good. In fact, the rabbis charged the early Christians as being deficient because they, ideally, did not marry and have children.

Chain Supersessionism: From Asherah to Secular Humanism

In one of my rabbinical school classes, we learned about how the goddess Asherah permeated ancient Israelite culture. I loved the idea that she is "mine" by spiritual or ethnic heritage. She belongs to my people and the land from which my people sprouted. What was most remarkable to me was the implied story of the suppression of this earth-based, embodied, fertility-focused spiritual consciousness in the "minority report." It was clear that parts of the Bible itself were a polemic against the widespread practices of Goddess-worship. The biblical authors must have imagined monotheism and more abstract notions of God (never to be represented in the material world) as an evolution whose time had come.

As such, it might have been the first instance of supersessionism, the practice of trading in a primitive religious sensibility for a more modern, enlightened one. Maybe all subsequent supersessionist moves were patterned after this one—an iterative process of clamping down on anything embarrassingly superstitious, supernatural, bodily, particular, earthy, emotional, or feminine. From there it's a one-way trip: YHVH-God supersedes Asherah; the social justice ideals of Amos and Isaiah supersede the festivals and sacrifices of the Temple in Jerusalem; the Maskilim supersede the Mitnagdim and the Hasidim; the Reform Jews supersede the Conservative Jews; the Christians supersede the Jews in general; the Protestants supersede the Catholics; the Unitarians and secular humanists supersede the Protestants. Each new self-satisfied generation imagines itself as having finally achieved escape velocity from the murky, muddled ignorance of the past. Each erases and replaces the last.

But each new iteration of enlightened freedom comes, I believe, with an equal measure of loss. Through the process of supersessionism, we abandon a vital part of ourselves. We tell our collective child self that there is no room for them in the adult world—that they must be silent while the reasonable grownups solve our problems. We forget that the child self is closer to the Source and so is the keeper of wisdom that we need. Through our arrogance, entire dimensions of reality get excluded from polite society. The mystical experiences and deep insights of our ancestors get relegated to the dustbin of history. The ecological teachings are dismissed as antediluvian. And we are left with a worldview comprised of thoughts that have just occurred to us in the last fifty years or so.

The Agency of *Adamah*

The centrality of the physical world in Jewish tradition doesn't mean that the tradition ignores metaphysical dimensions of reality. On the contrary, the mystical tradition of *kabbalah* recognizes four worlds, each emanating from God, and only one of them is primarily material. There are many passages in the scriptures, especially in the psalms, that evoke the intense experiences of God's spiritual presence or absence in our lives. Some of the prophets, like Ezekiel, report psychedelic, numinous experiences. But the tradition as a whole addresses us as material beings living in a material world. The vast majority of the commandments in the Torah are actions that we take or don't take with our bodies—do not steal, leave the edges of your field unharvested, do not work on the Sabbath. Theologically, as I read it, the physical is understood to be our mammalian access point to larger realms that include and transcend the physical.

Even more than this, all the layers of reality, physical and nonphysical, interpenetrate. In the biblical tradition as well as other religious and Indigenous traditions, the material world is not inert; it is animate. It acts with us, without us, and sometimes through us. In Western societies, we tend to imagine that we make decisions and take actions as individual rational thinkers. Our bodies merely obey the dictates of our minds, groups make decisions by counting the votes of individuals, and the earth is the object that is acted upon by human subjects. Despite the fact that this understanding is being disproven by the social and biological sciences (and known to be false by advertisers and pollsters), it is still the prevailing model because the ideology of individualism is essential for a consumer economy.

In the Torah, agency is distributed differently. In its narratives, our bodies act, we act collectively, and the earth acts. *Nefesh*, *am*, and *adamah* are agents in their own rights. They each make "decisions" and take "actions." Biblical language is full of intermingled references to bodies and emotions, "inner" and "outer." Intentions and bodily actions are often indistinguishable aspects of the *nefesh*. When God is angry, it simply states that God's nose gets hot. When Moses is resisting God's call to confront the Pharaoh, he explains that he is "slow of tongue."

Hebrew letters themselves, which are loaded with spiritual significance, are based in bodily images. The word for mouth is *peh*, which begins with the letter "*peh*," which looks like a stylized mouth. The word for eye is *ayin*, which begins with the letter "*ayin*," which looks like a stylized eye. We could say that our body parts have "minds of their own," but in a sense that would serve to reinforce the dualism—as if there is a mind inside of and separate from the nose or mouth. It may be more accurate to say that in the biblical texts, our noses and mouths—our bodies in general—are sentient. They act meaningfully in the world. Another way to put it is, as Boyarin asserts, that we are our bodies.

We see a dramatic illustration of this in the Genesis story of Jacob being tricked by Laban. The story goes that Jacob offers to work for Laban for seven years in exchange for the privilege of marrying Laban's younger daughter, Rachel. He puts in the seven years of work, which go by in a flash because he loves Rachel so much. But on the wedding night, Laban tricks him and gives Jacob his older daughter Leah instead. In the dark, presumably, they consummate the marriage, and Jacob believes he was with Rachel the whole time. But "when morning came, there was Leah!" (Incidentally, this is the origin of the custom of the groom checking under the veil to make sure he's marrying the right woman.) It doesn't matter that Jacob intends to marry Rachel, nor that he believes he is marrying Rachel, nor that there was an agreement that he would marry Rachel. Jacob's body has gone through the wedding ritual and the consummation with Leah, and so he is now married to Leah.

In our day, such a marriage, based on deception, would be instantly annulled. Someone would probably get sued, and that would be the end of it. Our law and ethics revolve around the inner states of intention and choice, not what the body happens to do for reasons unrelated to intention. To be clear, intention does factor into biblical law—murder and manslaughter are treated quite differently, for example. And in Jewish tradition generally, *kavannah*—focused intention— is an essential ingredient in prayer and ritual. But it is our physicality that tells the truth of who we are.

The *am* is also understood as an agent in Jewish tradition. The Ten Commandments, spoken directly to the people from the top of Mt. Sinai, are addressed to the people in second person singular—as if they are one being. The people as a whole is responsible for keeping the commandments and will collectively incur blessing or curse. The people recoils and the people speaks.

And most clearly, *adamah* is a sentient character with agency in the Torah. In the Genesis creation story, when the earth brings forth plants, seeds, creeping animals, and wild animals for the first time, the verb used to describe this bringing forth—*totzei*—is a feminine causative form. The feminine earth herself births these new beings. Leviticus warns us to not defile the land, or the land will "vomit you out." And the Sh'ma prayer, recited by observant Jews twice daily, warns that if we go astray and worship other gods, the earth will not yield her produce. A rabbinical classmate of mine, Daniel Delgado—a Quechua/Jewish writer and activist—teaches that Torah posits a three-way relationship between God, people, and land. In the scenario described in the Sh'ma, the people breach the covenant, God responds by closing the skies, and the land responds by withholding food.

In the same vein, Delgado points to a fascinating anonymous ancient Hebrew text called *Perek Shira*—Chapter of Song. In it, all the natural elements of creation sing God's praises. From the waters to the thick clouds to the sheaves of barley to the rooster, they all vocalize their teachings and warnings to us humans. They are all actors in the great drama along with us. In each of these cases and many others, it is *adamah* herself, along with her elements, who are the agents of action.

This ancient depiction of a live-wire world where bodies, collectives, and natural elements all act with agency accords with my own intuition about how life works. There are wild forces operating all around us all the time—many sentient streams crisscrossing and colliding, each with their own urges and their own wisdom. The Western image of us humans as the "deciders," uniquely able to act on a passive world, misses something essential. In my own life, even big decisions have not ultimately been made through a rational, individual process. In any struggle to make a decision, a point has always come when I've recognized that the decision was already made—maybe long ago—and I just needed to recognize it and embrace it. I've come to see reason as a relatively primitive instrument. From our gut biome to ancestral voices, we are awash in an ocean of sentience, and we need only to tune in to it.

The Nigerian-born philosopher and psychologist Báyò Akómoláfé speaks persuasively and beautifully in challenging the Western myth of the individual rational agent. He suggests that we may need an "ontological mutiny" to destabilize it. He invites us to acknowledge, instead, the many shifting layers of animate forces that shape us at every moment. In an interview with Joshua Michael Schrei, Akómoláfé asks, "What strange cocktail of Feline Toxoplasma and five-spice, what shudder of a passing breeze, what twilight fluttering of a hummingbird moth's wings set the thoughts in motion that architected the trajectory of your life's inspiration?" I hear this as a call to humility and surrender before the larger forces of which we are only a part.

Kundalini

One of the most profound spiritual experiences I ever had was also an intensely physical experience. It came during a yoga class in Chicago while I was in divinity school. As background, I had felt weighed down for years by a general sense of inadequacy; negative thoughts and feelings would churn relentlessly in my head. At the conclusion of the yoga class, we were lying down flat in "corpse pose," letting tension drain out of our bodies, and my thoughts were swirling as usual. But this time, a new thought-image began to form—that underneath the outer layer of this person and these patterns that I was so tired of, there was still a radiant, pure, innocent child. I would now call it in Hebrew my *nekudah tovah*—a shining inner pinpoint of goodness. That child is what I really *am*; the rest of it is just gunk, layered on by my society and the experiences of my past. That child is my God-self.

This realization started to become visual, as if it were projected on a screen above my head. I saw the spiritual gunk like a layer of tar. And underneath it was a glowing, beautiful, white light—unaffected by the layer above. In a flash, this light moved off the screen and reappeared in my solar plexus, glowing, and I could *feel* it. It was hot—intensely hot. It began to grow and spread throughout my body. It felt like something was taking me over that was both completely foreign—outside of my control—but also profoundly familiar, profoundly me. *This is what I really am.* The feeling was beautiful and frightening, and it filled my arms, legs, toes, eyes, hair. I felt sure that if anyone had looked at me, I would have been glowing like an alien. I was sweating from the heat of this light in my body.

It only lasted a little while—only until I started wondering how long it would last—but the experience affected me profoundly. I felt that it had been an experience of the knowledge of my own true nature. This knowledge informed a theology that I hold to this day—that we humans *do* manifest a divine spark, beautiful and loving and powerful. It does not stand apart from our physicality; it includes our physicality. We are essentially whole and good, along with the rest of creation, as God declares us in Genesis. I remember leaving the yoga studio and walking down the street feeling invincible. Through the yoga practice, my *nefesh*—my ordinary physical–spiritual self—had stuck a fork into the divine outlet.

This story would be unsurprising to any serious yoga practitioner. The *asana* practice—the physical poses that we often associate with yoga—is a technique for opening up the divine flow. Kundalini yoga in particular has this down to a science, having developed detailed understandings of how energy moves through the spine and how different postures evoke different energies. Kundalini Tantra teacher Swami Satyananda Saraswati explains it like this:

> Since the dawn of creation, the tantrics and yogis have realized that in this physical body there is a potential force. It is not psychological, philosophical, or transcendental—it is a dynamic potential force in the material body. And it is called kundalini. This kundalini is the greatest discovery of tantra and yoga. Scientists have begun to look into this . . . only rediscovering and substantiating what yogis discovered many centuries ago. The seat of kundalini is a small gland at the base of the spinal cord. . . . Those people who have awakened this supernatural force have been called rishis, prophets, yogis, siddhas, and various other names according to the time, tradition, and culture.

In other words, the great prophets and holy people of our world are those who have learned to channel and express the divine flow through their mammalian bodies: some through words, some through touch, some through art, some through acts of courage, determination, and self-sacrifice.

Pe'ah—The Wild, Holy Edge

The biblical tradition is rooted in the agrarian culture of a people living in the Levant around the tenth century BCE. They were acutely aware of their dependence on God's natural abundance, and the texts center wildness as a spiritual-ecological principle. The Garden of Eden itself is described as a wild paradise. The text (Genesis 2:9) says, "And God caused to sprout from the earth [*adamah*] every tree that was desirable to the sight and good for food, and the tree of life was in the midst of the garden" and a river (which branched into four) "to water the garden."

The Garden of Eden may have been envisioned as a fertile mountaintop from which flowed the four rivers and the nutrients that nourished the whole world. The tree of life in the middle of the garden was the archetypal Source from which everything emanates. This coincides with the image of the Asherah (sacred tree) as the great Goddess and life giver, attested by even more ancient Semitic traditions. We humans were part of that emanation from Eden and were formed from the same ground as the trees. God formed the *Adam* from the *adamah*—the earthling from the earth—and blew the breath of life into it.

As the Israelites escaped from slavery in Egypt and prepared to build a new society, the commandments they received—613 by rabbinic count—not only stipulated the just treatment of other humans but explicitly prescribed ways of caring for the land and our fellow creatures. The books of Exodus and Leviticus lay out these principles in delicious detail. Shabbat is sanctified as a day of rest for everyone, from the heads of households to the children to the "stranger" (immigrants) to the ox and the ass. No agricultural work is to be done, and so the land rests, "unproductive," one day out of every seven.

Building on this concept, for one year of every seven—the *shmita* year—the land is to lie fallow for the entire year. There is no planting and no harvesting. Fences have to come down from around one's fields because any volunteer crops are to be made available to everyone, explicitly including wild animals. For one year, the land reverts back to its natural state in which, as described in Genesis, all the green plants are food for all the animals, including humans. The soil is allowed to regenerate, and the wilderness is allowed to encroach and temporarily reclaim some of the land. It is as if God hits the reset button on creation.

The margins of the week and of the seven-year cycle are designated as holy time, and holy means wild. The land is naturalized, de-domesticated. There may well have been a practical understanding of the agricultural value of allowing land to lie fallow and regenerate. Indeed, Leviticus promises fertility and abundance if the *shmita* year is observed and warns of desolation if it is not. But a parallel set of commandments in Leviticus having to do with leaving edges wild in the realm of space (rather than time) suggests that there is something beyond the practical going on here. Farmers are to leave the edge (*pe'ah*) of their fields wild—"And when you reap the harvest of your land, you shall not reap all the way to the edges of your field, or gather the gleanings of your harvest" (Leviticus 23:22). And men are to leave the *pe'ah* of their hair wild: "You shall not round off (cut off) the edges of your head" (Leviticus 19:27). (This is the origin of the long, curly sidelocks that some observant Jewish men wear to this day.)

I love these teachings and the mystical principle embedded in them: that the divine manifestation can never be fully controlled. We can cut and harvest and shape our world to an extent—even to a large extent—but we should never try to contain it all. There is something living and breathing at the *pe'ah*. We should never try to suppress its volatility. The edges are wild, and the wild is holy. On the physical plane, this means a humble recognition that we humans do not own the land and we may not use it unlimitedly or abuse it. (Indeed, in Leviticus 25:23, God explains, "For the land is *mine*; you are just strangers and sojourners with me.") On the metaphysical plane, it means that the edges of our lives should always be left wild, open to God, allowing for a bit of indeterminacy, creating space for serendipity and for purposes beyond our understanding. The wild parts of the earth are holy, and the wild parts of ourselves are holy. They must be given voice. Once again, land, body, and self are united.

Rounding the Edges with Color-Coded Stickers

In the biblical prohibition against rounding off the edges of one's head (meaning hair), the word translated as "head" has the same double sense in Hebrew as it does in English. One's head can mean one's mind—do not round off the edges of your mind. Don't carve up the world into neat categories with rounded sides. Don't excise the uncomfortable and the contradictory. Rather, embrace the spaces, the relational zones, the gray areas, the shadow, the wispy fringe, and the hairy complexity—because this is where the spiritual juice and the wildness reside. I fear that the fecundity of these in-between wilderness spaces is getting lost in our world today.

I was struck one summer by a new protocol in progressive circles that sanitizes these in-between spaces. At both the Unitarian Universalist General Assembly and the Jewish Renewal movement's annual Kallah (respective denominational conferences, both of which I attended), conference attendees were encouraged to wear green, yellow, or red stickers on their lanyards. These stickers indicated the wearer's consent to one of three different levels of touch or proximity: green meant that hugs were welcomed; yellow meant ask before approaching; red meant keep your distance. Three primary colors in a simple shape, these stickers were intended to reduce misunderstandings and eliminate the need for self-assertion by those who find it difficult. I understood that these were pandemic-era adaptations; people with comorbidities needed to be able to communicate their vulnerability *before* someone leaned in for a hug, not after.

But it seemed to me that there was something beyond health concerns at play here. Many of us no longer feel that we are part of an *am*—a people with a shared history, experience, and vernacular. And so every new interaction is assumed to be a tabula rasa with no ground for mutual understanding. In the era of political polarization, "me too," deepfakes, and the constantly shifting sands of acceptable speech, people have become increasingly wary of each other. And in the era of social media and text communication, research has shown that our skills at reading body language and subtle emotional signals have declined. We have been losing confidence in our ability to encounter another human and communicate. In light of this social unease, we may welcome clear-cut signals, like traffic lights, to tell us what to do and to speak for us. (I even caught myself feeling a little relieved when I would see an acquaintance with a green sticker because I then knew the rule—it was okay to hug them.) We employ formal mechanisms to simplify our relationships.

But in reducing the possibility of misunderstanding and promoting safety, we may be paradoxically feeding an opportunistic virus of different sort: the virus of alienation from one another, the virus of rounded-off edges. This sticker protocol that was meant with all good intention to ease human interaction might also be reifying the notion that we are mutually unintelligible. We suspect already that relational encounters are too complex for us to handle on our own, the institution implicitly concurs by supplying the stickers, and so it becomes even more true. The gulf between us becomes uncrossable except through artificial mediation. The lanyard stickers perpetuate a kind of social infantilization that reinforces while compensating for our loss of relational skills.

These seemingly innocuous stickers exemplify the decline of our ability to handle complexity of many kinds. Sacred information contained in interpersonal nuance is getting lost; rounded down to simple shape-concepts that any five-year-old could understand. The natural range of human cultural and religious expression, with the rich, pregnant weirdness of its interstitial spaces, is being replaced by a system that I think of as "digital." It's as if our immersion in the world of computers has created habits of mind that carry over to the real world.

Digitized, Disciplined, and Domesticated

One of the hallmarks of digital rather than analog information is that analog information is "continuous," where digital information is not. If you imagine the sound of a saxophone, it may include a sweeping glissando or a warm vibrato that expresses infinite pitches between two notes. An analog recording, like an LP, reproduces the waveform of that full slide in the melody. Nothing is left out. A digital recording, on the other hand, translates the sound into numerical data, breaks the slide down into distinct microtones, and the pitch steps up or down from one to the next. This happens at such high speed that the human brain can't detect the steps, and we interpret it as a continuous slide. But some music aficionados can feel the difference.

I once had the privilege of taking a class with Dr. Hankus Netsky, a scholar and performer of Ashkenazic music—the Jewish music of Eastern Europe (think klezmer or "Havah Negilah"). As he taught his students to enter the subtleties of this music, he impressed upon us that the heart of this music is vulnerability. In performance practice, this vulnerability is expressed in part by the vocal sob (a tear-filled voice catch) and by melodic slides, especially downward slides. He said, "the audible reaching up in a measured way and then sliding down is the essence of Ashkenazic prayer."

The emotion, history, and spirit contained in these nuances are ineffable and cannot be quantized.

The difference that musicians hear between analog and digital sound, I believe, is the fullness and holy wildness of the spans in between the notes, at the aural edges. They say a record sounds warmer and more natural than a CD, and that's because it is. Even if we don't consciously know it, we sense a kind of impoverishment when those delicate in-between pitches are scooped up and assimilated into the nearest microtone. So much richness is lost. In mathematics, I'm told, this is known as a Voronoi partition, where you have a bunch of points (S) sitting in a continuous space, and you map every point in that continuous space to the S point that it's closest to. So the complexity of the continuous space gets reduced to the simpler set of S.

Similarly, when two people encounter each other, *there is naturally an infinite range of relational possibilities.* By reducing this infinite range to just three, as with the three lanyard stickers, we digitize our relationships. In the name of safety, we are sanitizing the in-between spaces, erasing mystery and wildness at once. We scoop up all the subtle variations in meaning and relationship and force them to conform to one of three options. This may seem like much ado about three stickers, but these stickers are emblematic of a much larger phenomenon.

For example, on the left, we have come to approach race in the same way. We divide the world into "Black," "brown," and "white;" or even "people of color"/"BIPOC" and "white," collapsing the specific heritages and ethnicities of the world's peoples into easily digestible categories. In Isabel Wilkerson's luminous work *Caste: The Origins of Our*

Discontents, she recounts a conversation with a Nigerian-born playwright:

> "You know there are no black people in Africa," [the playwright] said. Most Americans weaned on the myth of drawable lines between human beings have to sit with that statement. It sounds nonsensical to our ears. Of course there are black people in Africa. There is a whole continent of black people in Africa. How could anyone not see that? "Africans are not black," she said. "They are Igbo and Yoruba, Ewe, Akan, Ndebele. They are not black. They are just themselves. They are humans on the land. That is how they see themselves, and that is who they are.... They don't become black until they go to America or come to the U.K.," she said. "It is then that they become black."

All of society—including its *pe'ah*, its wild edge—is getting digitized, disciplined, and domesticated in the mode of the three lanyard stickers. A food court in a mall features a set of fast-food restaurants (S) that purport to offer authentic cuisine from different parts of the world. At the "Chinese food" service counter the semblance of authenticity is reinforced with faux-Asian graphic design elements in the employees' uniforms and the large menu screen, perhaps featuring chopsticks and a font that evokes the (English speakers') notion of Chinese characters.

Next door you can find the same thing, but with "Mexican food." These foods, served in Styrofoam containers and loaded with the exact same corn oil and sugar as McDonald's, can be delicious. But they bear little resemblance to food in China or Mexico (except insofar as world cuisines have come to imitate their American imitations). The complex and multidimensional cuisines that have evolved over thousands of years from lands and peoples around the world are scooped up and boiled down to a few simple alternatives, like colored stickers, all keyed to the American palate. In this way, world cuisine gets digitized.

In recognition that today's more urban, educated, Gen Z or millennial consumers may not be fooled by the food court model and may demand a greater experience of authenticity, the market has generated companies like WoodSpoon, which I noticed advertising in NYC subways a while back. Through the WoodSpoon app, you can order "home-cooked" meals from virtually any cuisine. In this case, the disconnection from the origins of those cuisines is offered as a benefit—a feature, not a bug. One WoodSpoon ad reads: "It's like getting grandma's soup without the questions about your love life."

In this ad we are promised the *feeling* of connection—grandma's soup with the sense of warmth and love and nostalgia that comes with it. But for a small price, we can sever that good feeling from the messy *obligations* of connection. Grandma's prying questions about our love life, her interest in the continuity of the family line, and the family knowledge and heritage are cut out of the equation entirely. We are liberated from the entanglements of the *am* while still receiving a simulation of family's comforts.

Another ad reads, "What you eat in Hong Kong is what you eat on WoodSpoon." This ad celebrates a philosophy of dislocation that would once have been seen as nonsensical: the idea that place *doesn't* matter. You don't have to invest in Hong Kong, or live in Hong Kong, or have ever been to Hong Kong to enjoy food that supposedly tastes identical to food in Hong Kong. This company seeks to erase distance and give the customer the fruits of a particular piece of land and culture without requiring a connection to that land or culture. In one of my favorite books, *The Ecology of Eden*, Evan Eisenberg comments on this phenomenon: "Woman and man have tasted the fruit of cosmopolitanism, a fruit that tastes like Anjou pear on Monday, kiwi on Tuesday, lichee nut on Wednesday, and Cape gooseberry on Thursday. It's a taste that is easily acquired."

This is all well-documented, the process by which corporate capitalism appropriates and commodifies the "volunteer crops" that spring naturally from the land and the *pe'ah* of human culture. The ability to quantify and render things modular is a boon for efficiency, and efficiency is everything. Youthful revolutionary fervor is compressed, processed, and marketed back to us in the form of t-shirts, accessories, and bumper stickers. Political pressure gets siphoned off and business booms. The 1960s movement to return to natural food systems grounded in small family farms today has become Whole Foods—a multinational corporation, owned by Amazon, that is intent on quashing competition from small farms and businesses through its sheer market power.

The benefits of this market-driven process of digitization are obvious: We get a global cornucopia of food available for low cost—the "fruit of cosmopolitanism" (although we know that the true costs of such foods are displaced). We can get at least a simulation of family nourishment without flesh-and-blood entanglements. We get to sample cultural treasures, past and present, and we get transported virtually around the world with no effort on our part. The reductionist ideology that may have started out as just a marketplace efficiency is now being hungrily adopted by the culture and applied to everything from interpersonal relationships to public policy decisions.

But cultural expressions (be they cuisine, music, text, dance, or art) cannot be severed from their roots in family, land, and community without losing something essential—even holy. Eisenberg writes of the connection between land and culture:

> As I sit at my desk, snow is falling outside; Sibelius is playing on the stereo inside. As plainly as snow is born of clouds is this music born of snow. From the spruce forests of Finland to the red deserts of Australia, every landscape in which humans have lived has sent up its characteristic shoots of song. Conversely, every novel, poem, painting, and play has roots, at however many removes, in a landscape (or several).

The implication is that food, land, culture, bodies, words, and music all evolve together. When we uproot the food, music, and so forth from their landscape, the further we carry it away in space and time, the more it loses what made it itself to begin with. But what is lost is rendered invisible to us who are already disconnected and dislocated. How could we sense the lack of depth when we too are uprooted and have nothing to compare it to?

Wildness

As much as I believe that we can find holiness in all materiality, not all matter is created equal. I love to walk down to the Hudson River, which is just a few blocks from where I live in New York City. I go out onto a pier and breathe deeply the semi-fresh air, look north toward the George Washington Bridge and the Palisades on the other side, look south toward the Atlantic Ocean. There are boats, apartment buildings, and seagulls, industrial effluvia floating in the water, and a very occasional fish. Sometimes I get a brief whiff of ocean. In my prayer life I try to embrace all of it with awe as God's cascading emanations—waves of first-, second-, and third-order creations. On the cosmic level, a fish and a plastic bag are equal members of the kaleidoscopic opulence of what is. But on an earthly scale, I'm aware that much of this urban panorama is a dead end on the tree of life. Unlike a fish, a plastic bag will never sustain anything, feed anything, or contribute to anything greater. What makes a river truly awesome is that of it which is wild. Its wildness is its true wealth.

The physical wild is the lifeblood of our planet, and there is no substituting for it with words, symbols, or ideas of human grandeur. *All* of life, no matter how many degrees of separation removed, flows from the wild spaces and natural processes of the earth. Where humans have remained enfolded within these natural processes and even contributed to them through sustainable hunting and farming practices, practicing reverence and care, there has been harmony. Humans have thrived along with all the other creatures of the earth.

The Lenape people lived in the northeast of what is now the United States for 12,000 years. The Hudson River was then known as Muhheakunnuk—the river that flows both ways—because the people were acutely aware of its process and role as a tidal estuary. Salt water and ocean creatures flow up for many miles, bringing life inland, while fresh water from the mountains flows down, carrying mineral-rich soil and nourishing the riverbanks. Fish migrate back and forth, and some wildlife lives only in the in-between zones. The bank of the river was truly a bank for the Lenape people. It held riches and jewels in its liquid vault—it offered abundant food and materials for clothing and trading. It was a highway to faraway places. The current was currency. Water was wealth; water was life. Like good fiduciary stewards of a river bank account, the Lenape people used what they needed and saved the rest. *Adamah* supplied the interest, and life continually regenerated.

The first European colonists in North America reported finding indescribable abundance. In 1493, Christopher Columbus wrote admiringly of what he found in this world that was new to him. He wrote that the land was

> full of the greatest variety of trees reaching to the stars.... Some of them were in leaf, and some in fruit; each flourishing in the condition its nature required.... There are also wonderful pinewoods, fields, and extensive meadows; birds of various kinds, and honey ... and the excellence of the rivers, in volume and salubrity, surpass human belief, unless one should see them.

As he wrote these words, I wonder if he could have imagined that his very presence there heralded the beginning of the end of that abundance, along with the survival of many of the peoples who had nourished it for generations.

I do not mean here to idealize the first peoples in these lands—they were flawed humans just like us today and guilty of greed sometimes, just like us. There are stories of overfarming and overhunting. The Native American artist and teacher Carol Lee Sanchez describes a cycle, recounted in the oral histories, in which the native peoples of North America "deviated from their Sacred Ways and became greedy," and then realized the damage they had done and returned to connection with the Mother Earth and Father Sky. But it is no coincidence that the land was abundant, biodiverse, and thriving after 12,000 years of the first peoples' tenancy on it.

Nor it is coincidence that the same land has been dangerously desecrated in the 500 years' tenure of peoples who considered themselves more "advanced" and have been benefiting temporarily by an overdraw on the account.

In an ironically insightful observation, Columbus may have inadvertently hit on the reason why the land was so healthy. He wrote of the native people he encountered: "They do not practice idolatry; on the contrary, they believe that all strength, all power, in short all blessings, are from Heaven." The native peoples, in living interdependently with all the creatures of the land, recognized their utter dependence on God's blessings. They recognized the "spiritual" and the "physical" as inseparable. The Cherokee engineer and educator George Thomas said, "I feel science is actually a natural thing for Native Americans because of our relationship to the Earth, our spiritual beliefs, and respect for The Creator's great laws . . . It's not just an academic pursuit for us; science and theology are one and the same." Accordingly, each act of taking from the earth had spiritual significance. It was sanctified with ritual, reverence, and gratitude and reciprocated with giving.

Idolatry is a complex concept that, for some people, smacks of dusty, hidebound religion. It's generally used in Jewish and Christian traditions to refer to the worship of anything other than God as if it were God. It has been misused at times on the religious right to apply to the worship of deities in other religious traditions. (In most traditions with multiple deities, devotional practices engage the deities as access points or portals to connect with the One. Christ functions this way for some Christians as well.) But in the Ten Commandments, idolatry refers to the creation and worship of a representation of *anything* in the natural world—in the skies, the earth, or the waters. Representation is a form of control, and the natural world, in its wild state, is sacrosanct. To represent it is to objectify it. To objectify it is to limit it. (For the same reason, it is prohibited to represent God, including by uttering God's ineffable, secret name.) Wealth flows abundantly from the natural world, but we are to worship the source of that abundance and not the product of it.

With this understanding, it was in fact the Europeans who practiced idolatry, worshipping the wealth that could be extracted unwillingly from the land and the people who lived there. A theology of separateness from the natural world laid the groundwork for its instrumentalization. The humans credited themselves for their own prosperity (a kind of self-idolatry), while the earth was reduced to a "resource," a thing. Aldo Leopold, widely considered the "father of wildlife ecology," put it this way: "There are two spiritual dangers in not having a farm. One is the danger of supposing that breakfast comes from the grocery, and other that heat comes from the furnace."

The colonists fell prey to these spiritual dangers. They became alienated from the earth and therefore from their own nature as part of it. It's not hard to see from here how this artificial separation extended to other creatures and then to other humans. The native peoples were seen as just a (dispensable) element of the land. Those without the power to prevent their own objectification were reduced to "human resources." From here, this delirium of alienation reached its nadir in the kidnapping and enslavement of Africans. It was a short leap from 1492 to 1619.

Valuing the Invaluable

A few years ago, *The New York Times Magazine* produced a fascinating series that placed the history of slavery in this country at the center of the American experience. The series is called "1619," which is the year that the first enslaved Africans were brought to this land. The concept is that it was *that* moment, not 1776, that was the true founding of America. The article called "Capitalism" by Matthew Desmond is a stunning account of how the values and technologies developed during slavery directly gave rise to the kind of capitalism we have today—a capitalism that, compared to other nations, is extreme in its brutality and its destructiveness to the earth, air, and water on which we all depend. This is not just how capitalism is—it's how *American* capitalism is.

In the article, Desmond describes how the workers were forced to work the cotton fields at breakneck speed every day of the week for every second that there was enough light to see. Their overseers developed sophisticated systems for measuring and tracking the productivity of each worker for each hour in each section of the field. They devised algorithms to determine how much each worker should be able to produce in a day. The farms became more and more efficient, and more and more cruel, as the managers tweaked their systems, revised their techniques, and learned how to squeeze out ever-increasing productivity. Long before the digital world of computers, they digitized and codified the life energy of human beings.

Those cotton plantations were the progenitor of today's factories, farms, and e-commerce warehouses. The technology is more advanced and the coercion less brutal, but the surveillance of the workers, the use of algorithms to maximize productivity, driving the minimum wage earners to produce more and more in each hour—it's all echoes of the same thing. And while today's so-called "unskilled" workers are paid and are theoretically free to quit, they are often so impoverished that they can't risk leaving. To be clear, it is not slavery, but neither is it a life, a living, or fair pay for a fair day's work.

Our disconnection from the land, our separation from *adamah*, may have begun here as well. As it turns out, the cotton plant is a ravenous plant that sucks vast amounts of nutrients and water from the soil. Desmond writes, "A field could only tolerate a few straight years of the crop before its soil became depleted. Planters watched as acres that had initially produced 1,000 pounds of cotton yielded only 400 a few seasons later." And so the owners were faced with a problem: how to keep profits growing. The solution? Acquire more land. No letting the soil lie fallow; no crop rotation; no *shmita* year; no *pe'ah* left wild. No. All of that would have lowered profits. More land.

More land could be gotten for next to nothing from the native people who were living on it. And so that's what they did. They bought forest land on the cheap—vibrant, nutrient-rich, biodiverse land—and made the enslaved workers clear-cut it, raze it to the ground. As John Parker, one enslaved worker, put it, "whole forests were dragged out by the roots." And so the great American forests were replaced, row after row, acre after acre, with the cotton monocrop. Later, chemical fertilizers and pesticides forced the dead soil again and again into a zombie fertility.

This abuse of the land also foreshadowed the capitalism of today where the natural world is simply wealth to be punctured and extracted by the syringe of cheap labor. If it gets depleted, force it or leave—and leave the stripped, barren land behind. A forest left as a forest was worthless. The colonial overlords didn't know what value a forest had.

I would suggest that we still don't know the value of a forest. Even though we theoretically get the importance of healthy soil, biodiversity, and the interdependent web of life, it's the habits of mind that developed during slavery that still guide our economy. Value is what can be measured. Value is counted in dollars and hours and pounds. Value is fungible—it doesn't have to take any particular form. It can be in the form of a worker, a number of dollars, or a piece of land. It's all the same. And value is a zero-sum game—if I have more, you have less; if you have more, I have less. Our culture churns humans and nature into capital. And today's ecological crisis exposes an economy so spiritually hollow that, trying to fill itself, it devours everything, even its own *adamah*-mother. Our society mistakes the invaluable for the valueless.

For the longest time I was confused about the word "invaluable." It seemed like it should mean "not valuable." But eventually I learned that in fact invaluable means you can't place a value on it. It's infinitely valuable—precious in a way that's beyond measure. Here we leave the domain of economics and enter the domain of religion and spirit, the region of the heart that is truly a parallel universe to that of profit-making. In this region of the heart, it is the invaluable that matters most. A human life is invaluable. The smile of a child who feels safe: invaluable. A recipe passed down in a family through the generations: invaluable. A shared moment with a loved one that becomes a shared memory: invaluable. Music, art, dance: invaluable. Human cultures: invaluable. A forest, an ocean, a clear sky that releases heat back out into the cosmos: invaluable.

Once we can begin to value differently, then we can begin to rehumanize our society. When we learn to value the invaluable, we will find that we are already wealthy beyond measure. And when we dwell in *that* wealth, we may begin to heal our society and our earth.

It's the Thought That Counts

At a UU congregation I served, a building renovation was going to require extensive scaffolding. A 50-year-old crabapple tree on the property was in the way of the scaffolding, and it was determined that the tree would need to be cut down. The staff and congregational leaders who were managing this project knew that this would be a delicate matter to present to the congregation—people had emotional attachments to that tree since it had grown there for so long. And so a plan was hatched to carefully explain the necessity of the tree removal to the congregation and then hold a ceremony honoring the tree before cutting it down. A congregant with a wood shop at home offered to slice branches into thin disks that could be given to people as mementos or sold at the church auction.

I expressed reservations about the idea of claiming any part of the tree for our human purposes when we were already planning to fell it for our human purposes. It seemed to me that we should be approaching this project with the humble intention of doing *teshuvah*—the Hebrew term for repentance and repair—making sure that the entire tree was returned to the earth and planting at least two trees elsewhere in its stead. *Teshuvah* is a religious concept that allows for atonement for wrongdoing. It allows for the nuanced understanding that an act can do harm even when it's necessary; it embraces complexity. But this congregation was essentially a secular context in which the idea that we would do a wrong that required atonement was hard to stomach. If it's necessary, it can't be wrong. My concern was overruled on pastoral grounds: Having a piece of the tree to take home would help people feel better about the loss of the tree (a loss that was understood as *our* loss rather than a loss to the earth and the tree itself). The ceremony would prevent any guilt and substitute an expiatory tone for compensatory action.

I led the pre-memorial tree ceremony. We all gathered around the tree with stories about the tree, prayers, poems, and songs. We thanked the tree. And after the service was done and the crowd dispersed, the chainsaw came out and the tree was felled as planned. What happened to the tree next is a little murky, but from what I was able to piece together, the wood shop guy took some of the branches home to turn into memorial discs, some of the branches were left in a pile for many months with a thought that they would be brought inside and sanded down for a different purpose, and a third portion was chopped up, bagged, and put out with the garbage. Much of the tree ended up in a landfill.

The impulse to honor the tree with a ceremony was a beautiful and wholesome one. And the more we learn about the sensitivity of trees, the more it seems possible that the tree was able to receive that love in some way. But it also seems that the ceremony, disconnected from any particular tradition of practice around ethical and spiritual dilemmas, had the unintended effect of serving as a substitute for restitution. It inadvertently blurred the reality that we were about to kill a living being who was a member of an interdependent ecological community (however diminished in New York City). Our act would further damage that small ecological community. And it failed to include acts for mitigating that damage. On the planetary scale, one tree is not a huge loss, but neither is it a loss that can be erased on the plane of words and ideas. The difference gets confused in people's minds; the semiotic plane, like the virtual plane, comes to feel real—sometimes it even supersedes the material plane. At our moment of ecological crisis, this misconception is a grave danger.

As we modern humans separate our own souls from our bodies, seeing our souls as the real self and the body as just a vehicle, we do the same with the *adamah*. The soul of the tree is honored, and the body is discarded. We have misty-eyed appreciation for "nature" while often participating in the demise of natural systems in the course of enacting that appreciation.

We enjoy images of the natural wonders of the world on our large-screen TVs (buying larger screens every year, currently averaging over 47 inches), forgetting that the TV is made from materials painfully extracted from the very ecosystems it depicts. Those of us with means may go on ecotourism adventures, burning untold fossil fuels in our travels, or drink (plastic) bottled water from faraway pristine springs. We carve nature up into lots so that each of us in the suburbs and rural areas can have a piece of it for ourselves (the wooden disc from the crabapple tree writ large). Meanwhile the energy use and extraction from the earth for each of these single-family homes and their green lawns destroys natural habitats at the site of the housing as well as ecosystems at the points of extraction. And all of it contributes to lethal climate chaos on the planet as a whole. We love the earth so much, like a child squeezing a puppy, we are killing it.

Words Create Worlds

I've noticed a growing awareness that land acknowledgments, de rigueur now in the progressive world, may function the same way as the ceremony for the crabapple tree. Although the initiative is truly well intentioned, by verbally recognizing the theft of land from native peoples and going no further, we risk performing a kind of empty self-absolution. Graeme Wood, for *The Atlantic*, writes,

> *Teen Vogue* put it well, if unintentionally: 'Land acknowledgment is an easy way to show honor and respect to the indigenous people.' A great deal of nonsense about identity politics could be avoided by studying this line, and realizing that respect shown the 'easy way' is just as cheap as it sounds. Real respect occurs only when accompanied by time, work, or something else of value.... Without time, work, or actual redress, the land acknowledgment that implies a moral debt amounts to the highwayman [robber's] receipt.

Wood goes on to quote Dustin Thmahkera, a professor of Native American cultural studies at the University of Oklahoma: "To acknowledge Indigenous homelands and to return those lands are related, but the former alone allows for rhetoric without further action."

I do not mean to suggest that words are impotent. I would not write if I thought they were! Words create worlds, as they say, and in the biblical creation story it is the speech-acts of God that constitute reality. Speech can form our cultural "agreements"—the consensus reality that we inhabit—and influence politics with life-or-death stakes. We have seen, especially in recent decades, how speech can congeal into action in sometimes wonderful and sometimes terrifying ways. Visionary speech by civil rights leaders have inspired courageous, transformative justice work; on the flip side, racist and anti-immigrant speech has inspired deadly terrorism. On January 6, 2021, the ephemeral world of ideas, emotional heat, glowing images on screens, and bits of digital data swirling by the billions manifested in the physical world—human beings storming the Capitol carrying Confederate flags and leaving behind five dead.

On that very same historic day, years of accrued speech propelled a Black man (Rev. Raphael Warnock) and a Jewish man (Jon Ossof) to the Senate in the deep South. A previously immutable reality in Georgia was breached by the power of ideas and spirit. It was a conflagration of countless liberationist energies—the inspiring words of the two leaders, the tireless work of volunteers who called and wrote to protect the rights of the people, and of course the wisdom of the voters themselves—that profoundly changed the material world. "The 82-year-old hands that used to pick somebody else's cotton went to the polls and picked her youngest son to be a United States senator," Reverend Warnock said about his mother. "The improbable journey that led me to this place in this historic moment in America could only happen here."

I remember feeling awed by all that transpired on that one day—the karmic consequences of speech. The word "transpired" comes from that Latin *trans-*, meaning "through," and *spirare*, meaning "to breathe." I'm awed by all that breathed through from spirit to matter, from words to reality. The barrier is so thin. If we learn nothing else from this era, we should learn that through our words, things transpire. These extraordinary moments showed how permeable the barrier is between the world of ideas and the world of action. Our words carry both huge responsibility and sacred opportunity for transformation.

Spiritual Bypass and the Caging of the Yetzer Ha-Ra

Along with the risk that facile DIY rituals and flowery language may substitute for real-world action, they also flirt with what some in the therapeutic communities call "spiritual bypass." John Welwood, the Buddhist psychologist who coined the term, explains it this way:

> Spiritual bypassing is a term I coined to describe a process I saw happening in the Buddhist community I was in, and also in myself. Although most of us were sincerely trying to work on ourselves, I noticed a widespread tendency to use spiritual ideas and practices to sidestep or avoid facing unresolved emotional issues, psychological wounds, and unfinished developmental tasks. When we are spiritually bypassing, we often use the goal of awakening or liberation to rationalize what I call premature transcendence: trying to rise above the raw and messy side of our humanness before we have fully faced and made peace with it.

This "rising above" the messiness is yet another way of describing our decampment to the virtual and symbolic worlds. We inadvertently deny real life—our bodies, our earth, and our earthly troubles. We also sometimes keep our relationships shallow, choosing to hover in a "no drama zone" and make detours around the hard and sometimes painful work of relationship.

I fear that much of what passes for spirituality today in the secular, spiritual-but-not-religious, New Age, self-help, motivational, and even pop religious worlds risks falling into this "spiritual bypass" trap. We soothe ourselves with the trappings of spiritual language. We dabble in religious and cultural traditions that immediately feel good or that evoke pleasant nostalgia for our childhoods. We pore over social media to learn correct political vocabulary. We busy ourselves with discourse. Echoing Boyarin's old argument between the Christian Fathers and the rabbinic Jews, we believe we don't have to literally keep commandments or do things with our bodies; it's faith, intention, and "the thought" that matters.

It is a growing trend among younger generations, especially in the progressive world, to eschew romantic partnerships, marriages, and families—and all the difficult entanglements that come along with them—in favor of the "chosen family." People I've known who have gone this route often have many friends with whom they have a range of relationships—semi-romantic, semi-sexual, semi-practical, semi-supportive. They have no aspiration for marriage (and bristle at the suggestion that they should), but rather distribute their needs for connection among several people in a diversified relationship portfolio. Polyamory is celebrated as a "love that liberates" from oppressive relationship norms. But as monogamy fades as a shared value within the *am*, and nouveau forms of relationship rise in its wake, confusion and grief seem to be also rising.

A friend of mine tells the story of her nephew, Pete, who found himself in a polyamorous trio—dating a woman who was living with another woman in an open relationship. By my friend's account, Pete and his girlfriend had a very sweet friendship, which may or may not have included sex. But they talked all the time, cooked together, even took a class together. This was all with the consent of the girlfriend's other partner. This delicate relational balance came crashing down quite suddenly. The girlfriend's partner became uncomfortable with the arrangement and demanded not only that her girlfriend and Pete break it off, but that he go over to their home and publicly end his relationship with the girlfriend.

Pete was stunned to find out that his girlfriend was okay with this plan. But to express hurt or anger toward his girlfriend (or her partner) in this situation would be to violate the progressive ethos. In entering a polyamorous relationship, Pete had been hoping to counter the toxic masculine code of "ownership" of one's partner. The emotions of jealously, possessiveness, and anger belonged to that code, and to succumb to those feelings would be a failure. He had hoped to take a spiritual bypass right over them. But of course he did feel those things for very natural evolutionary reasons. He understandably *was* hurt and angry that his girlfriend, with whom he had had a loving relationship, was casually agreeing to break up with him at the demand of another lover. But as my friend tells it, he had trouble admitting this to himself. Instead, he felt confusion and shame at his own outmoded longings. Pete couldn't understand why he felt so terribly sad.

Meanwhile, as the bonds of more conventional couplehood are fraying, sexual images—particularly those of half-clothed women—are everywhere. All sexual desires are celebrated as equally valid, with some even lauded and defended as the foundation of marginalized sexual identities, "polyamorous" being one of them. Gender is understood as a fluid thing. We can identify as any gender and have sex with someone of any gender. We might be attracted to people of all genders, which my kids inform me is to be "pan," that is, pansexual. There is to be no judgement when it comes to sex and sexuality.

With so many options and so few restrictions, you would think that everyone would be having sex and lots of it. But the results are in, and ironically our libertine, sex-saturated society is generating much *less* sex. There has been a dramatic decline in all kinds of partnered sex over the last twenty years (only masturbation is on the rise). Correspondingly, there has been a precipitous decline in fertility rates around the world. Some suggest an economic explanation for this—people can't afford babies—but it seems that there's more to it than that. Religious people consistently have more children than nonreligious people, and it's not because religious people are richer.

How could this be? How could today's liberated socialites get less action than the Victorian prudes of old? It seems that progressives and young people today are applying the it's-the-thought-that-counts ethic to sex. We're doing a kind of collective spiritual bypass, where we celebrate "sexuality" as performance and identity, symbol and empowerment, but when it comes to actual sex with all of its sticky mess, we can't seem to get it together. The ubiquity of pornography as well as the soft porn of commercial and social media has the paradoxical effect of a kind of exposure therapy. Nakedness ceases to be exciting, and eroticism is drained from the culture.

Additionally, since the old rules of romantic engagement have vanished and we are not all yet wearing colored lanyard stickers to broadcast our preferences (although there are certainly attempts to codify dating protocols on college campuses), we don't really know how to do it. Heterosexuality in general is suspect these days, presumably because of the power differential inherent in it. The #MeToo movement has highlighted the dangers of romantic and sexual contact such that everyone is a bit wary. Sex itself is presumed guilty until proven innocent, oppressive until proven liberatory.

In a well-intentioned attempt to protect LGBTQ+ or vulnerable individuals from what's seen as repressive heteronormative expectations, progressive culture gives strong pushback against the very notion of "natural" and "unnatural" sexuality—even the suggestion that we are sexual beings by nature. In progressive ideology, we are *nothing* by nature—everything we are is constructed. With this belief, "asexuality" is now an official sexual identity recognized by the American Psychological Association (which, to me, exposes the whole roster of modern sexual identities as a slippery continuum to the erotic vanishing point). Sex and family formation are not to be celebrated as a vital part of life; they are merely consumer options, equivalent to others and value neutral.

Bumble's Blunder

Any public figure or company today ignores this creed at their peril. When the dating website Bumble launched what was supposed to be a humorous, tongue-in-cheek ad campaign to prod women to not give up on finding love on their platform, they fatally misfired. They quipped: "A vow of celibacy is not the answer!" In other words, sure, men can be cads, but don't retreat to the nunnery; engage in the world of sex, love, dating, and partnership anyway. This was profoundly offensive to Bumble's clientele. The ad was construed as shaming women into engaging in sex with abusive men. The backlash was intense, and Bumble quickly figured out that they had to do damage control.

Bumble had to remove the ads and make a donation to the National Domestic Violence Hotline. They ran an apology on Instagram that recited the perspectives they had heard: "from those who shared that celibacy is the only answer when reproductive rights are continuously restricted; from others for whom celibacy is a choice, one that we respect; from the asexual community for whom celibacy can have a particular meaning and importance which should not be diminished . . ." and others. Bumble had violated a cardinal rule of the progressive world: never question a person's choices, or suggest that one ought to do anything, especially in the realm of sex.

Choice in progressive circles is sacrosanct, and nowhere more so than around sex. We should not only be free from rape, harassment, and pressured sex (which, of course, we should), but we should also be free from the grandmother who hopes we'll get married, the pope who teaches the Catholic faithful to welcome children, and the humorous ads of a dating site that wants our money. Especially those deemed most vulnerable are entitled to freedom from even a shadow of influence from anyone. Bumble's apology referenced this ethic: "For years, Bumble has passionately stood up for women and marginalized communities, and their right to fully exercise personal choice. We didn't live up to these values with this campaign and we apologize for the harm it caused." We are imagined to be so fragile that a dating website's advertisement can "harm" us. In a strange puritanical throwback, the public discourse around sex must now be clean and polite, even timid. And if we want to bypass sex altogether, that is our sacred right.

But for all the admirable intention here of protecting people from abuses of power, I believe that something holy and irreplaceable is lost when sex is completely tamed. Sex is the generative power of the universe. The explosion of orgasm is a fractal of the big bang—the divine masculine and divine feminine coming together in creative combustion, the thesis and antithesis spawning synthesis. It contains the potential energy of both terror and ecstasy. The drive for sex is imprinted in our DNA as the deepest evolutionary imperative. It is an animate force emerging directly from the depths of our *nefesh*. Sex is not just a consumer lifestyle option like any other. Sex is radically different from everything else in life. More than with anything else, the *pe'ah*—the edge—of sex must be left wild or it will die.

My favorite story in the Talmud concerns the value of our *yetzer ha-ra*—our "bad" inclination or desire:

> The ancient Sages decided that they were going to capture and imprison the Yetzer HaRa. So they ordered a complete fast of three days . . . whereupon he [the Yetzer] was surrendered to them. He came forth from the Holy of Holies like a fiery lion. . . . He [the Yetzer] said to them, "Realize that if you kill me, the world is finished." They caged him for three days, then they looked in the whole land of Israel and not a single egg could be found.

When society cages our *Yetzer*, digitizes it, and reduces it to a set of polite, bland political agreements, life loses its vitality, and we lose our own fiery essence. The *Yetzer* is "bad" sexual desire, but it's also the urgent force of desire itself. With the *Yetzer*, the world lays eggs, builds cities, makes art, grows food, and births children. With the *Yetzer*, we have the ever-unfolding emanation of new life and creativity, pleasure and passion, bubbling and surging like a fountain from the Garden of Eden. Without the *Yetzer*, we have sclerosis—and a slow cultural and spiritual decay. We bypass life itself.

Decadence

A relative of mine lives at the intersection of 77th Street and Central Park West in New York City where the Macy's Thanksgiving Day Parade begins. Each year he sends me and my family an invitation. We flash this invitation on our phones, and it slips us through the barricades at the police checkpoint. The kids squeeze through the crowd to get the best view possible (they're short, so we let them), and we stand there at the corner taking it all in. We each play our roles: the kids are excited; my husband is bored; I am appalled.

Last year, as the peacock display of corporate capitalism unfurled before our eyes and the crowd cheered (but a bit perfunctorily), I newly understood the word "decadence." I've learned from the writings of the brilliant columnist Ross Douthat that "decadence" has two meanings: Most commonly it connotes something luxurious, self-indulgent, and hedonistic. But it also encompasses the word "decay," referring to something that is deteriorating and fading. This parade was both.

On one hand there was the proud celebration of the corporate brands that capture the world's imagination—Disney, McDonald's, Pokemon, and of course Macy's itself.

Macy's evokes a vague, hope-filled pseudo-spirituality with its one-word tagline, "*Believe*," rendered in a whimsical script with a star as the dot of the "i." These brands that made us misty eyed as they rolled by represented billions in consumer spending, untold tons of petroleum extracted from the earth, the sweatshop suffering of humans, the factory farm suffering of other animals, and square miles of landfill piling higher each year. The giant helium-filled balloons in the shape of the beloved characters themselves—Mickey Mouse, Ronald McDonald, Snoopy, and so many others—cost Macy's $190,000 each to make and then $90,000 per year to maintain. That makes a year's balloon tab alone $1,950,000. Decadence.

On the other hand, the parade had the smell of a food just beginning to spoil. As if its remaining vitality was just residual from a former glory. The crowd was lackluster. There was a smattering of applause; some cheering, more or less halfhearted depending on who was rolling by. In a particularly galling attempt to whip up some energy, the announcer chanted, "When I say *Macy's*, you say *Parade!*" "*Macy's!*" "*Parade!*" "*Macy's!*" "*Parade!*" (You may recognize this as a common protest chant pattern—as in, "When I say *climate,* you say *justice!*") The announcer was straining to appropriate the energy of the resistance movement in service of the very thing it is resisting. But it didn't work. The energy remained flat. My son later told me that he made himself hoarse cheering and yelling, trying to compensate for the spiritless crowds because he felt badly for the marching bands. Decadence.

Despite the subdued reception by the crowd, to suggest that the $1,950,000 spent on inflating corporate brands into balloon creatures might be better spent elsewhere—say, helping restore rainforests destroyed by those very brands—is heresy in our culture. For one thing, a couple mil is a drop in the bucket for corporate America. *You should see how much X corporation spends on Y*, I'm admonished. *This is nothing.*

More importantly it is unthinkable that this tradition should be abandoned because the Macy's Thanksgiving Day Parade is a high festival of the religion of corporate capitalism. It infuses the transactional shopping experience with meaning. The cheering for the giant balloon characters is a rite of devotion. And the balloons are unmistakable as idols. The various characters are here before our eyes, timeless, larger than life, in their absolute platonic form. Their sheer size as they float above us in the sky makes them awe-inspiring.

We invest our hopes in these corporate idols. We invest in them a lost vitality, childhood innocence, a capacity for play, nostalgia for a simpler time, a world where our differences dissolved in the universalizing river of furry bubbles of softness. (We may not have Walter Cronkite any more, but at least we have Pikachu.) These idols float—the balloons float, the floats float. There's even, inexplicably, a giant floating acorn. They bear none of the weight of real life; they float above, bypassing it all. But they also bring no *actual* vitality, innocence, play, moral clarity, or peace. They are empty and impotent, as are all idols. The balloons rise not because they are filled with the *ruach Elohim* (the breath-spirit of God) but because they are filled with helium, literally lighter than air, less than nothing, like the virtual world utterly insubstantial.

Along the sidelines, parents were buying normal-sized balloons for their children, hoping to take a piece of the magic home with them. And so bouquets of helium balloons got released, accidentally yet inevitably, and we all watched with vague regret as they drifted in up into the sky, knowing that they would soon sink into the ocean and join the rafts of floating, choking plastic—perhaps the Great Pacific Garbage Patch, already twice the size of Texas. Decadence.

Granted, the feeling of shared celebration surrounding the parade can be a truly joyful thing. Indeed, any time a group of people gather for a live event (a sports game, a concert) it can evoke a rapturous sense of communion. This is no different. And as a further concession to those who love this parade, I will admit that I love the marching bands. Despite their militaristic origins, hearing the music approach from the distance, then fill the air with that warm brass sound, the talented young musicians from around the country playing their hearts out, and then watching and hearing it recede down the street—it is moving, even for me.

And even for me, the yearning for normalcy in a world upended by disintegration of every kind is strong. Many of us are hungry for signs that "normal" still exists, that everything will be okay, and that we're still living on the same planet that we lived on in 1924 when this parade began. So a shared event with all the familiar symbols of continuity, including even Santa Claus, can be deeply satisfying. It meets a need and brings comfort and enjoyment.

But that enjoyment requires denial, and so it comes at a cost. In the words of a Hasidic elder from the TV show *Shtisel*, it's like lighting a cigarette off a burning Torah scroll. We must be honest that this parade is not Macy's act of altruism, rolled out for our uplift. It's a vital diplomatic mission for corporate capitalism itself—so vital as to be worth millions of dollars and to need defending by police snipers and bomb-sniffing dogs. I can't help but think that to gather in celebration of an economic system that lays waste to people and planet helps perpetuate that system. And the group exercise in idolatry helps buttress the power of the idols for everyone.

But the culture of consumption symbolized by the balloons and floats has failed us, and on some level we know it. It's all beginning to deflate. The decadence is becoming visible. And in what feels like a bit of wry cosmic humor, apparently the world's natural supply of helium is running out. (The helium shortage has become so severe that Party City has had to close dozens of its stores.) Even the great idols, inflated with less than nothing, turn out to be unsustainable. The jig is just about up.

The time is at hand for us to rediscover something real to "*Believe*" in. If we want to recapture our spirit of innocence and play, great—let's invite Sabbath into our lives and play for one whole day out of seven. If we want the joy of communion with others, let's build community where we live, connecting with people not through brands but through shared faith, heritage, work, or music.

If we want magic, instead of a floating, plastic acorn, let's find a real acorn. Though a thousand times smaller, it dwarfs its balloon imitation. It is a miraculous thing—a compact, elegant form encasing the seed of the majestic oak tree, all its potential energy pulsing inside it. A being so small and so potent, bursting with life like a divine clown car. When I hold an acorn in the palm of my hand, I know it is real. Nothing decadent. Integrity. Durability. The force of transformation. It is vibrating with the *ruach Elohim*. An acorn is something in which we can truly *Believe*.

Breasts

Breasts have great symbolic and psychic power. The breastfeeding mother is an archetype of nurturing love that crosses religious traditions, cultures, and eras. The iconography of the "nursing Madonna" depicts Mary nursing the baby Jesus in thousands of paintings and sculptures. Hindu sacred imagery depicts the great mother goddess Durga nursing her child, the elephant god, Ganesh. In Jewish tradition, one of the names for God is El Shaddai—"El" meaning God, and "Shaddai" meaning mountains or breasts. A symbol of this particular name of God graces every *mezuzah,* marking the doorway to a Jewish home. In literature, art, and liturgy, the love of the divine feminine comes through the maternal act of nursing. There are, of course, a million ways that God's love can and does get transmitted from person to person. And there are a million ways that it travels through a parent to a child. Breastfeeding is only one. But it is one with powerful resonance, perhaps because throughout most of human history, it was a matter of life or death.

We know that breastmilk has all the nutrients that babies need to grow (which is why we humans evolved to crave the tastes of fat and sweetness). It's in our genetic makeup. The *only* way an infant could survive was by the milk of a mother. It was an essential element of the life cycle.

In this way we were exactly like all other mammals, from mice to elephants to blue whales. Our bodies have the miraculous ability to transform what would be inedible to our young—be it grass, a peanut butter and jelly sandwich, or a freshly killed ibex—into the one substance that they most need.

But in some difficult situations, thanks to modern medicine, women and trans men can and do sometimes choose to have their breasts surgically removed. A woman may have a mastectomy to remove cancerous or potentially cancerous cells. For trans men and some nonbinary persons, this surgery is known as "top surgery," an elective surgery usually done to align one's body with their gender. Breasts may mark them too visibly as women. I would not presume to judge the necessity of this action for an individual—and indeed for some people I have known with excruciating gender dysphoria, gender-affirming care can feel nonoptional. But I have come to believe that there are certain choices that are important for individuals to make for themselves but that also, as a widespread trend in society, point to deep-seated spiritual grief and alienation.

Zooming the camera out, what does it mean for a society as a whole if more and more people are removing their breasts? This is, in fact, a current trend in the United States, as reported dispassionately by the *New York Times*. The absolute numbers are still tiny, of course, but as a matter of meaning in our culture it feels significant. As it becomes more socially acceptable to change one's body to align with one's identity, as the *nefesh* is conceptually split between physical and spiritual, more people are taking advantage of many kinds of surgical options. But breast removal is in a category of its own, quite different from, say, nose jobs. I wonder if there are larger cultural currents at play here. To the extent that we've built a culture in which a growing number of people remove their breasts, we are severing that connection with our animal selves and our animal siblings. No other mammal that we know of would voluntarily relinquish its own capacity to nurture new life.

Today, someone who removes their breasts and still wants to have children has more options than they would have in the cave. Perhaps their partner has the ability to bear and nurse the child, or perhaps they can prevail upon a friend who has recently given birth. More likely, however, they plan to rely on infant formula to feed their baby. Many mothers who have breasts rely on formula anyway for a host of reasons—preference, inability to nurse, workplace policies that make it impossible, or the difficulties of a culture that is hostile to nursing mothers. And of course for parents who adopt their babies, formula can be essential. I myself, by necessity, supplemented nursing with formula for my twins—and I was beyond grateful to have that option.

Starting in the 1940s, doctors and formula manufacturers began promoting formula as a safe and even preferable alternative to breast milk. It was part of the ethic of "better living through science." Breastfeeding has been in decline since then, to the point that when there was recently a shortage of infant formula due to supply chain problems, it became a nationwide emergency. Formula is the perfect product from the viewpoint of capital because it is "price insensitive," meaning if customers need it, they need it, and they're going to buy it no matter what the price. A mother who does not breastfeed her baby is the perfect customer because she unquestionably needs it.

Breastfeeding has, however, enjoyed some periodic rebounds over the last decades, due to either liberal or conservative activism. The "attachment parenting" movement and lactation advocacy and support groups like La Leche League used to be sites of overlap where certain crunchy, nature-loving liberals and certain religious conservatives found themselves aligned, strange bedfellows though they were. Today, however, as with so many issues, polarization has forced realignment. In my circles, most progressives these days are much more vehement about affirming a mother's free choice to nurse or not nurse without judgment. As part of a rejection of any "shoulds" in society, they are highly attuned to the danger of mothers feeling guilted or pressured by the discourse of "breast is best."

Now we have the mirror image pair of bedfellows: choice-oriented progressives aligned with business-oriented conservatives. On the progressive side, there's an ideology that mothers' relationships to their children should be able to be more like fathers' relationships—free of bodily entanglements. All parents of any sex or gender should be equally capable of feeding and caring for their infants. When such symmetry is not found in nature—because it's only the female mammal who makes milk—we demand synthetically produced symmetry. And the business conservative is more than happy to oblige.

American culture and finances dictate that our biological reproductive lives should only interfere minimally in our economically productive lives—or our self-actualization, for that matter. And so our babies are often fed formula, sleep trained by any means necessary, and sent to paid caregivers at the earliest possible opportunity. (Affordable or free childcare is considered a justice issue because it is assumed that parents will need to or want to work, and in the absence of any family or "village" to take care of their children, they will have to outsource childcare.) For the poor this is by financial necessity, and for the wealthy it's by "choice," although the pressures of the meritocracy sometimes make it feel like necessity. As a society, we don't have time for babies.

Maternal Grief

Mothers whom I have known often experience profound grief when they have to leave their infant in a daycare facility. I remember a phone call with a congregant, Rachel, who was a single mother of a baby girl. She was distraught because she had recently had to go back to work as a public school teacher and take her daughter to a daycare facility. It was excruciating for both of them. She insisted that she knew she was lucky compared to other families. Cobbling together maternity leave with the summer break, and a newly passed law that allowed for up to six weeks of medical leave (without pay), she had been able to delay the inevitable for a total of four and a half months. Many people she knew only got six weeks. But time had run out, and it still felt far too early.

Rachel had been exclusively nursing her baby, and she knew that at daycare the baby would have to use a bottle. Rachel regretted not having practiced the bottle with her more. The caregivers reported that the baby wasn't drinking from the bottle. And it was clear: she was always hungry and crying when Rachel picked her up. They tried different kinds of bottles with different nipples to no avail. It felt to Rachel that something was fundamentally wrong here. She said, "I am being paid to care for other people's children, while other adults are being paid to care for my child. I'm at work, tired, knowing that my baby is hungry with strangers. It's like some cruel kind of torture."

She also felt a great sense of loss in descending from the intimacy of caring for her daughter 24 hours a day, where she knew her ins and outs, and every breath, and every tone of cry, to being what she called a "part-time mom." It felt deeply unnatural to Rachel that she was now spending more time at work, which she confessed she cared little about at this point, than with her own child. This perspective flies in the face of the ideal of career orientation that is supposed to be empowering for women in the progressive worldview. But this was Rachel's truth as she experienced it in her *nefesh*, which was naturally deeply intertwined with that of her daughter. Parents like Rachel can sense the spiritual damage unfolding, but through economics, ideology, and cultural expectations, they are hardlocked into a commodified world.

The Ideology of Infant Formula

Infant formula solves many problems at once for both progressives and conservatives: It creates parity between two parents or between family and paid caregivers—all can feed the baby equally. The child's unique physical dependency on the biological mother can end at birth rather than continuing for another year or more. The mother can fulfill her nurturing responsibilities to her baby indirectly through the medium of money (for formula) rather than directly through her body. The biological mother is no longer uniquely capable and responsible; she can physically extricate herself as she chooses. Without the project of nursing, she can return to work sooner, more easily, and without the need for workplace accommodations. Careers can resume faster. Crucially, corporations can demand more from their lowest-paid workers. In fact, it is now wealthy women who more often have the "luxury" of nursing their babies and poor women working minimum wage jobs who can't afford it.

Formula gives the U.S. economy the boon of an industry worth over $4 billion a year. Globally it is worth $38 billion, and the U.S. government has been hell-bent on protecting this industry from its natural competitor. In 2018 a resolution from the World Health Organization to promote breastfeeding in developing countries, and to limit the advertising of formula, was attacked by the U.S. government. The United States threatened Ecuador, which had introduced the measure, with punishing trade measures and withdrawal of aid unless they dropped it. After all, the argument went, we shouldn't deny formula to poor women who "need" it.

In fact, in developing countries especially, formula can be dangerous for babies—it does not provide the same immune protection as breast milk and often has to be made with unclean drinking water. It also costs money, and once a baby is drinking formula and a new mother's milk dries up, there is no going back. It can exacerbate poverty. So the industry uses aggressive tactics to pressure women in developing countries into dependency on formula, spreading misinformation about breastfeeding, giving free samples, and leaning on doctors to recommend formula. The cynicism of this breaks my heart. For the enrichment of multinational corporations, we humans—not all of us and not always by choice—are replacing miraculous natural nourishment with inferior synthetic nourishment.

I'm sure the industry could counter all of this with statistics that show that formula saves more lives than it costs. One could probably argue about this forever. But it is undeniable that formula shifts the center of power from people to corporations. It interposes a product between the mother and baby and between God and the mother. The flow of love as expressed through milk naturally comes through the mother, but it can't, and so it flows through the product. And perhaps this begins a lifetime of trying to find love mediated by products. We take this as normal. Our experience of love gets derailed as it detours through a piece of clothing or jewelry, a car, a new gadget, a computer or device. We learn to accept love indirectly, via corporations, rather than straight from the source, human or divine.

I can feel as I write this also the passionate critiques: The romanticization of the mother–child bond and the nursing relationship is regressive. If formula is formulated to give babies all the nutrients they need and it gives so much freedom and flexibility to parents, the argument goes, the only possible objection to it would be that it gives so much freedom and flexibility to parents. The idea of "the natural" has been used for millennia to oppress women and sexual and gender minorities—it has been deployed to lend authority to the structures of patriarchy. Anything that reifies the idea that biology is destiny takes us back hundreds of years in our progress toward human liberation.

There is truth in all of this. And the impulse to protect the gains that have been made is itself a holy impulse. I also detect here a current of grief, however, bubbling up from my generation and younger generations who were raised with a dearth of what is in fact "natural"—an orientation toward our young that is built into the design of our bodies and has been instinctively practiced by all mammals including humans through the ages until very recently. The angry response to the idea of the natural being better is one borne of grief—that we never had that, and rather than admit it as a loss and try to change it, we angrily say that we didn't need that anyway and look at all the measurable benefits.

We use the expression, "I drank it in my mother's milk" to mean that something is so primal, so foundational, so essential to our experience of love that it is part of us. What does it mean if now, instead of our mother's milk, we drink Similac's milk? What does it mean when our first taste of life does not come from our mother but from the factory of a multinational corporation? Our connection to our bodies, our mother's bodies, and to the natural systems of the earth begins to fray early. Alienation becomes part of us from birth.

Collateral Relatives

This system also creates alienation among our collateral relatives. A collateral relative is a relative descended from a brother or sister of an ancestor. If you look back far enough, all nonhuman animals are collateral relatives to humans, having evolved with slightly different DNA from the same prehistoric ancestors. We humans have always had a mixed relationship with our nonhuman cousins—sometimes collaborative, sometimes competitive, sometimes eating them and occasionally being eaten. But in modern times our relationship with nonhuman animals has become horrifyingly one-sided. Our own troubled relationship with the natural ebbs and flows of our human bodies causes collateral damage to other species. And this, in turn, causes collateral damage to the ecosystems that depend on a delicate balance of all its creatures.

For all other species and for premodern humans, our current orientation toward our young—in which we have to fit caregiving around our busy schedules—would be unimaginable. Evolutionarily speaking, the nurturing of young is not a detour or a diversion but the prime directive of life. Everything else has to adjust around this all-consuming project in the same way that the organs in a pregnant body get moved and squeezed to make room for the growing baby in the womb. If humans oriented around our young the way other animals do, our collateral relatives would be left unmolested, at least for the purposes of providing food for our infants.

But rather than surrender to our mammalian design (as we do during pregnancy without a choice in the matter), at the earliest possible opportunity we modern humans take control and mechanize the process. And in order to mechanize the process of feeding our young, we have to harness and mechanize the reproductive processes of our cousins, mostly cows. Most—though not all—infant formula is made using cow milk. I won't describe here the continual suffering endured by most dairy cows and their calves in modern factory farms. But it is the violent severing of the relationship between bovine mother and infant that makes possible our human lifestyle choices. Our own alienation ripples outward and imposes alienation on other species.

This is not to suggest that the domestication of animals for food is a modern phenomenon. Early humans also domesticated cows, goats, and sheep—we drank their milk, made yogurts and cheeses, and occasionally ate their meat. But the scale of this animal husbandry was tiny—intended only to provide for a family or small group of families. In ecological impact and cruelty, there is no comparison to today's mass production of milk products in which the animals are merely "stock" that happens to be "live." In the small farms of premodern times (if a couple of goats in one's yard can be called a farm), there was an intimacy and a two-way relationship between the humans and their collateral relatives, even when that relationship ended with an eventual slaughter.

Is this an idealized picture of the relationships between ancient people and their domesticated animals? I would have suspected so, except that we still see examples today of just such relationships. In some small farms around the world, the humans treat the animals with great care and sensitivity, tending to their health and well-being and, in the case of dairy animals, protecting the mother–infant relationship.

I have witnessed this firsthand at the goat pastures of Isabella Freedman, a Jewish farm and retreat center in Falls Village, Connecticut. All day the mother goats nurse their kids in an open field. At dark they are brought into the barn, and mothers and kids are kept in separate pens overnight. First thing in the morning, the farm workers bring each mother goat into the milking shed and milk her by hand. They thank her for the milk, and she is released into the pasture with her kids. Within a few minutes, her body has made more milk, and they are nursing again.

One might wonder if it matters for the farmer to thank the goat for the milk when the goat has not chosen to give it and can't understand human words anyway. I would think that it matters very much: Rather than an attitude of entitlement to take something from one's "live stock," thanking the goat promotes an orientation of humility and gratitude. It acknowledges that the act of milking intercedes temporarily in a holy relationship between the goat mother and kid conveyed through the milk itself. This pair—a tiny web strung with milk—is a single unit of the web of life. And for the mother goat, the tone of the farmer's orientation toward her is palpable. Anyone who has lived with a nonhuman animal knows that most meaning is conveyed with tone and body language and even, mysteriously, through thoughts that never get intentionally conveyed. (This is true of humans as well—when people are speaking, most of the meaning gets transmitted to the listener nonverbally.)

A relatively humane system of animal husbandry like this one can only happen on a small scale. It is labor intensive and requires the farmers to know the animals individually. Such a system could never supply all the current formula needs of the world, not to mention dairy production in general. So I would suggest that the scale at which it's possible to raise animals humanely and with minimal impact to the environment is the scale that should dictate how much dairy the world consumes. My guess is that, just as asparagus breaks at just the right point so that the tough stem is naturally identified, the amount of dairy available when produced at a humane scale would be just the right amount for people who really need it. Mothers who physically cannot nurse, parents of adopted babies, and children and adults who need dairy to address a health condition would all have what they need. Perhaps there would also be enough for others to also enjoy dairy on special occasions.

Whether this would in fact magically work out exactly like this, I don't know. But I believe that the principle is sound: Let us humans find the humility to live within our means—to only take from the *adamah* and her creatures what can be taken with sensitivity, care, and gratitude. Take only what can be given with relative ease, without the rending of relationships or the pollution of land, water, or sky. Assume this as our baseline and figure out from there how to meet our actual human needs. Perhaps if we did this, we would wind up reuniting not only cows and calves, but human mothers and babies. As society reorganized around the natural cycles of raising our own young, the primal maternal bonds could be rewoven. The kind of loss and grief experienced by Rachel and her daughter could become a distant memory. It could be a holy return to body and land for everyone.

Being Worthwhile

A congregant, we'll call him Trent, emailed me to request a pastoral meeting. In his email, he first reassured me that he wasn't suicidal, and then wrote the following:

> What I've been struggling with is whether it's okay for me to exist. I was given up for adoption at birth, and adopted by a family that saw me as a burden. Especially now with so much discussion about reproductive rights, which I'm very much in favor of, it's hard not to see my very existence as a problem. I'd be a better political symbol and raise more money and attention for the cause as a difficult illegal abortion in Iowa in 1961 than I ever could give or raise or garner as just me.

When we met, he elaborated about how he felt he was using up resources the planet couldn't afford and receiving advantages (educational, financial, and otherwise) that might have been better used by someone else. My heart ached listening to him and hearing how he had learned to measure his own worth along such brutally utilitarian lines. By his calculations, his nonexistence would probably have benefited the world more than his existence. So he didn't deserve the space, food, and water that he received. By the metric of the meritocracy, he could not justify his life. He, as a person, was not worthwhile.

Unsurprisingly (to me, at least) his parents are stalwart atheists. They allowed him to explore various religious beliefs as a child but discouraged him from committing to one until he turned 18 and could choose—or not choose—for himself. This is an approach I've seen among Unitarian Universalist and liberal secular families as well. Give the child the menu and let them choose for themselves when they are ready. Treat religiosity as a controlled substance, like alcohol, or a dangerous responsibility like driving or voting. Children can look but not touch lest they be drawn in and carried away by irrational urges and emotion. They should keep a safe distance until they are adults and their brains have matured enough to provide them the inoculation of healthy skepticism and reason. At that point if they still want to adopt a faith, fine.

By that time, however (and this is almost certainly part of the strategy), the child's natural religious impulses have been submerged. They have formed a self without God, and they have gone through what would have been eighteen cycles of holidays without ritual, warm memories, or a connection to a spiritual community. At this point religion is just a series of intellectual propositions. They either believe it or don't believe it, but it's no more than that. One congregant bragged that his parents "cleverly" read him Bible stories interspersed with other myths and fairytales to ensure that he would find nothing special in the biblical stories. He would know that they are as silly as the tooth fairy—something to outgrow and maybe remember with a wistful smile.

Secular parents are often afraid that religious faith is so easily ingrained and so difficult to shed, they need to protect their children from it with these kinds of techniques. From my own experience I would say the reality is just the reverse: faith is easy to lose and hard to gain.

Faith is exactly Trent's struggle right now. He cannot believe in something unprovable—his own intrinsic value—because he can't feel it; he has not been supported in developing ways of knowing beyond the rational. And so he evaluates his value the same way we evaluate the value of a product—does its benefit outweigh its cost? Is it efficient? Is it attractive? Does it need repairs? Is it easy to set up and run, no assembly required? Is it low maintenance? Is it popular or desired by others? This icy materialism, when applied to people or other living beings, is soul crushing. More importantly, nobody can pass these tests because we are not machines. We require growth, not assembly; healing, not repair; nurturing and care, not maintenance. We are all inefficient and materially unproductive (except for farmers, but even there most of the work is done by God). Our worth lies in our holiness, which is immeasurable.

But the ideology of the meritocracy haunts us. It taunts: Are you worthwhile? How much do you have to achieve to make you worth not having been aborted? The people in Trent's progressive social circles inadvertently perpetuate his economic model of human value. They surely don't mean to do this and might be horrified by the thought, but their "rights"-oriented ideology has some unintended effects. In the case of adoption, for example, Trent explained to me that his pro-choice friends see adoption as a harmful phenomenon in society because it can serve as an enabling agent for pro-life polemic and legislation. The argument goes that since unwanted fetuses should be aborted, not carried to term and adopted, there should be no need for adoption (or at least not for infant adoption). The availability of adoption muddies the waters. And so every adopted person is a testament to a failed system—a flashing engine trouble indicator of a woman who should have had access to abortion but didn't.

As Trent tells it, adopted people in this social milieu are prompted to feel "almost guilty" for their existence and the societal failure that it denotes. He told me a story of a friend of his, also adopted, who posted on Tumblr about feeling badly about having been adopted because she knows that adoption gives fuel to the pro-life political agenda. Rather than getting the compassionate, supportive response one might hope for, her post was met with a chorus of agreement, people writing, "thank you for saying that and for understanding how problematic adoption is." I imagine these responses were as painful for Trent's friend as Trent told me they were for him.

Pregnancy

Without knowledge of divine delight, religious practices, or community support, it's understandable that someone like Trent would question what he was saved from abortion "for." There must be some grand purpose to justify his existence if it came at such a great cost—a woman unwillingly (he assumes) carrying a baby to term. It's inconceivable in this progressive worldview that a pregnant woman might be following her faith, her conscience, her heart, or her body in wanting to carry the baby to term. But pregnant women who are not in a position to raise a child in fact *do* make this choice for all of these reasons and more. We don't know Trent's birth mother's story. But I wonder—if Trent were able to imagine her as a woman who made a sacrifice out of love rather than as a victim of injustice, might he be better able to love and value himself? Might he feel that he is a person with a place in this world rather than a walking mistake?

The celebration of abortion rights is so vehement in the progressive world that it sometimes feels like pregnancy itself is suspect, whether wanted or not. With the need for breastfeeding obviated by infant formula, pregnancy is one of the few biological processes that still root us ineluctably in our bodies. Worse yet from a progressive worldview, pregnancy roots only *some* of us in our bodies—only biological females. It imposes a unique, nontransferable burden, limitation, and risk. It changes us. Organs are pushed aside to make space for the growing life within, and along with those organs, our priorities are often rearranged. The physical experience can dramatically recalibrate our sense of self. And to the extent that in the progressive worldview true liberation requires liberation *from* our bodies' constraints and obligations, pregnancy is by nature regressive.

Vivid expressions of this sentiment can be found readily on social media, as in this anonymous post I came across on Facebook:

> We need to reframe how we think about the uterus. The uterus is not a nurturing organ; it doesn't need to be. A fetus is frighteningly good at getting the resources it needs to nurture itself; if placental cells are implanted anywhere other than the uterus . . . they will rip through a body, slaughtering everything in their path as they seek out arteries to slake their hunger for nutrients . . . (it's no coincidence that genes involved in embryonic development have been implicated in how cancer spreads). Rather than a soft cosy nest, a uterus is a fortress designed to protect the pregnant person from the developing cells inside them. Because of our huge and (metabolically speaking) expensive brains, human fetal development requires unrestricted access to a parent's blood supply . . . The uterus has

> evolved to . . . eject the fetus before it develops enough to kill the host . . . Pregnancy is not a joke. It is a life-threatening event, a parasitic attack on a human body; just one we have romanticised and been desensitised to. The miracle of birth is that we have a specialised protective organ designed to, if all goes well, let us survive it.

Granted, the language in this post is extreme, and its hostile tone probably does not reflect the feelings of most pro-choice feminists. But extreme expressions can be useful in surfacing the deeper essence of a worldview. In this case, recasting pregnancy as a "parasitic attack" vividly conveys the feeling that the natural order, especially the process of human procreation, is threatening. Feminists and progressives are deeply invested in the independence of the self from the body (biology is *not* destiny), hence the insistence on nongendered language that separates childbearing from motherhood and even womanhood. But in pregnancy, that illusion of the independence of the self from the body collapses. Because pregnancy impinges on the integrity of the body, it inevitably impinges on the sovereignty of the self.

This is what I think of as a secular individualist understanding. Religious teachings, by contrast, tend to stress a more expansive understanding of the self. Christian scriptures teach of a fundamental oneness that underlies our individual selfhood: "There is neither Jew nor Greek, there is neither slave nor free, there is neither male nor female; for you are all one in Christ Jesus" (Galatians 3:28). In Jewish tradition, the self is located in the entire *am*. The community is depicted as having collective reactions and taking action collectively, and it is this collective action that bears consequences, good and bad, for all. In Hindu teaching, the Atman (individual self) dwells within the Brahman (cosmic, divine reality) like bowl of seawater in the sea; they are one and the same substance. Buddhist philosophy takes this yet further and teaches that there is no self to begin with. Buddhist meditation techniques help us to destabilize the illusion of the individual self, with its grasping, hungering self-interest, which is seen as the root of human suffering.

"His Body, His Choice"

In my experience in the progressive secular world, this perspective is common. Childbearing needs to be justified according to a cost–benefit analysis. Shortly after my conversation with Trent, another congregant reached out for a conversation with me, this time from the prospective parent side of the equation. Janet and her husband were weighing whether to have a child or not. She had an impulse to have a child, but she didn't want to give the reins to that bodily impulse. The idea of childbearing was romanticized anyway, she believed, and mostly through religious discourse. With no religious summons to "be fruitful and multiply," there were few reasons to have children and many reasons not to.

For one thing, she said accurately, the earth is already overpopulated, especially with American consumers. As white middle-class professionals, she and her husband would be in a position to give their child advantages that she believed no one should have. Adoption was also problematic in her view because it leverages the advantages of moneyed families to indirectly "buy" babies from poor women who can't afford to keep them. Janet's husband was very reluctant to have a child for all these reasons and was considering getting a vasectomy. She wished he would wait until they had come to a decision together but didn't feel that she could argue the point because, in the progressive ethic, his bodily autonomy was unquestionable even, or especially between married people. She had no right to try to influence his decision. She shrugged and said, "his body, his choice."

Family Planning

Abortion has long been a cause célébrè for both liberals and conservatives. But this issue, like the question of nursing and formula, slices our social movements diagonally, forcing the usual left/right columns to regroup. Most notably, it divides fiscal conservatives from religious conservatives, while aligning progressive activists with big business. Capitalism as a whole requires laborers and consumers, so you could argue that it always needs more babies. But overall, corporate America has benefited from the economic impacts of abortion: More women in the workforce means a greater supply of workers, and wages go down. The "family wage," which supports a family on a single income, is a thing of the past. Conversely, abortion restrictions tend to harm the economy. Research estimates that state-level abortion restrictions cost state economies $105 billion per year. Put simply, it has been said that capitalism requires abortion.

So many companies have publicly come out as "pro-choice," paying for their workers to travel out of state for abortions or paying legal fees for Lyft drivers who get sued as accessories to abortion. The availability of abortion allows female employees to work more like men. More work can get done with less interruption, and companies don't have to deal with expensive parental leave or pregnancy accommodations. It also allows women to have sex more like how men have sex, without the terror that a momentary lapse in judgment will have lifelong consequences. But there is a shadow side to this corporate enthusiasm for "choice." If you're a Lyft driver, the company may pay your legal fees if you're sued, but if you want to have a child, you're on your own. You don't get health insurance or paid parental leave. If you work at Amazon and get pregnant, you can count on still being required to lift heavy boxes and being denied bathroom breaks.

The fact that capitalism "requires" abortion should be a red flag. In the modern secular era, all of society has tilted away from promoting families bound by obligations to promoting lone rangers feeding the economic engine with ingenuity and long work hours unhampered by such obligations. If you could personify the economy, the economy *wants* us to live in a hyper-individualistic world, without ties of home, where the mighty bottom line drives every decision. Depending on our class, our financial fixation may be driven by necessity or by greed; the economy doesn't really care. But either way, pregnancy, childbirth, and childrearing are messy, unpredictable, values-shifting processes that are incompatible with it.

Some white-collar companies even will pay for employees to freeze their eggs so they can delay pregnancy and childbirth if they so choose. It's considered a "life hack for ambitious women." This is offered as a fertility benefit, but I suspect that these companies cynically calculate that it's low odds that the frozen eggs will ever lead to a pregnancy. (Some experts say that there's only a 2 percent chance that a frozen egg will become a baby.) It's telling that it was Silicon Valley companies that offered this benefit first, and that today they offer it almost universally. The tech industry is the nexus of the flight from the physical world and its bodily freightage in favor of the cool, clean liftoff to the virtual world. In this context, it only makes sense that the biological clock should yield to the digital clock.

Because of all this and more, American women are trying to have children later in life (which is great news for the multibillion-dollar fertility industry) and ultimately report having fewer children than they want to have. And about three-quarters of women who have abortions give financial necessity as the reason: "I can't afford to have a baby." Freedom of choice is somewhat illusory when economic pressures and powerful corporate interests are pulling our strings in every direction. These are the heartstrings of those who yearn to form families and care for their young in the noble tradition of all the creatures of the earth. The ethic of the secular left, with its emphasis on choice, sometimes misses the deeper truth that, sometimes, true freedom comes from a willingness to make sacrifices for a greater cause.

Sacrifice

Sacrifice is the third rail in American society. It's widely understood among leaders, especially politicians and liberal clergy, that to ask people to give something up for a greater cause is a nonstarter and can even prompt backlash. Attempting this was already a mistake back in 1979, when President Jimmy Carter gave the infamous speech mockingly called his "malaise speech." In it he talked about the materialism of Americans futilely seeking fulfillment in money and products. To address the energy crisis of the time, he urged Americans to return to an ethic of community, hard work, and collective sacrifice for a greater cause. He said:

> To further conserve energy, I'm proposing tonight an extra ten billion dollars over the next decade to strengthen our public transportation systems. And I'm asking you for your good and for your nation's security to take no unnecessary trips, to use carpools or public transportation whenever you can, to park your car one extra day per week, to obey the speed limit, and to set your thermostats to save fuel. Every act of energy conservation like this is more than just common sense, I tell you it is an act of patriotism.

The speech was panned and mocked, Carter lost his reelection bid, and no politician since then has gone within a mile of a cardigan sweater. Today, it is almost unthinkable to ask people to give up something for the public good. We see this in both conservative and liberal circles: Americans across the political spectrum get our hackles up when we are asked to make sacrifices. Almost nobody who can afford air travel has stopped flying in response to the massive amounts of fossil fuels burned by commercial flights. Almost nobody will take public transportation if they own a car and driving is a reasonable option given traffic, parking, and so on. And relatively few people have stopped eating meat despite the multiple environmental benefits of doing so. (Animal agriculture is responsible for over 14 percent of global greenhouse gas emissions.) This is to say nothing of the benefits to the meat animals themselves, most of whom live lives of great suffering.

We saw that in the height of the COVID-19 epidemic in 2020–2021, conservative communities in particular resisted social distancing and masking and later, vaccines—especially when paired with the word "mandate"—because these sacrifices felt unacceptably burdensome, regardless of who might benefit. (Liberal communities, including houses of worship, public schools, and arts institutions, were, in this case, generally more willing to cramp their style. Certainly, in major cities like New York City, the threat was real and terrifying enough to prompt personal compromises.)

But in progressive communities, during the years of my ministry, I found that sacrifice was often a nonstarter as well. To suggest sacrifices around food prompted particular resentment. Our connection to food is deeply emotional. It's connected through memory to family and comfort, romance and celebration. And some of the foods that cost the earth the most, like hamburgers, also happen to be the most delicious and satisfying. So I gingerly touched on this issue in my sermons from time to time, suggesting that moving away from meat could be a way to live more lightly on the earth. But despite how gently and rarely I brought this up, never preaching an entire sermon on the topic, congregants would complain that I preached on this theme "all the time." It must have sounded so gratingly loud in their ears when I mentioned it. And when a congregant proposed that the church's annual auction dinner be a gourmet vegan meal, there was practically an uprising.

This matter of the auction dinner was a case study in the notion of sacrifice in progressive communities. The congregant who had volunteered to serve as the head chef for the auction dinner suggested that it should be a vegan meal and proposed a menu that sounded, to me and others, delectable. When the organizers of the auction itself got wind of this, they responded with great consternation, saying that because this is a special fundraising event, the meal should be special as well, and that surely the auction would be less financially successful if the meal were subpar, that is, if no meat were served. They had a clear sense that the congregation would not take kindly being asked to sacrifice the pleasure of the kind of meal they were accustomed to. Presumably, people would either not come to the auction or would not spend as much while there. During the back-and-forth negotiations about this, I expressed my support for the chef's vision of the vegan meal and encouraged the organizers to stay strong on this as an expression of their Unitarian Universalist values. I soon learned that in so doing I had overstepped my bounds as a minister. I received a phone call from the president of the board taking me to task for failing to be sufficiently pastoral in the situation. I should not have been pushing these poor congregants into the boxing ring with each other; I should have been helping them find common ground with some kind of compromise position (a little chicken, perhaps, but also a vegan option?). I should have been less concerned with the outcome of the dispute and more concerned with making peace in the congregation. I apologized to the board president and to the other congregants involved. And there was indeed chicken served.

It was the same lesson I had learned long before with Clara and her dying husband: It was not my job as a minister to push my congregants to do the right thing (in each case, it was only the right thing in my personal opinion, not backed by any religious authority). It was definitely not my job to push them to make sacrifices. It was my job to make peace and validate their choices.

In Sohrab Amari's book *The Unbroken Thread*, he tells the story of the Catholic martyr Maximillian Kolbe who made the ultimate sacrifice: imprisoned at Auschwitz, he volunteered to take the place of another prisoner who had been selected for death by starvation. Kolbe was a priest who had spent his life serving others, campaigning against communism, militant secularism, and later, Nazism. During the Holocaust, he sheltered almost 2,000 Jews in his monastery. The story goes that at Auschwitz he continued his service, undeterred. He tended to people's souls, heard confession, and even fed people from his own ration. One day, when a prisoner was discovered to have escaped, ten men were selected to be starved to death as collective punishment. One man, when his name was called, cried out, "My wife, my children!" Kolbe stepped forward to take his place. It is said that after two weeks, when he finally died, "his face was calm and radiant."

Amari writes about this story:

> What gripped me the most, what I couldn't get out of my head once I learned about Kolbe, was how his sacrifice represented a strange yet perfect form of freedom. . . . Kolbe climbed to the very summit of human freedom. He climbed it—and this is the key to his story, I think—by binding himself to the Cross. . . . His apparent surrender became his triumph. And nailed to the Cross, he told his captors, in effect: *I'm freer than you.* In that time and place of radical evil, in that pitch-black void of inhumanity, Kolbe asserted his moral freedom and radiated what it means to be fully human.

Amari makes the case that although it may sound backward to modern ears, freedom is not the ability to fulfill our appetites, seek pleasure, and avoid pain; it is precisely the power to sacrifice those things when necessary for something larger than ourselves. Hopefully most of us will not be called upon to make sacrifices as excruciating as Kolbe's, but we are all faced with choices every day between what we want in the moment and what might serve the greater good; between the small ego self and the vast divine Self.

Religious practices of all kinds, from dietary laws to Sabbath-keeping to prayer and devotion to charitable giving, are small sacrifices designed, in part, to strengthen this muscle. As our connection to *adamah* and to *am* grows stronger, and our sense of self grows to encompass more and more of the world, we may find that our desire to take from others diminishes. We now feel part of the sacred whole from which we might have been tempted to steal. And our desire to give increases—as we are part of that to which we give. In this way, the grief of our isolation may subside and the joy of connection may grow.

Bicycle-Powered Light Bulbs and Sand Mandalas

Meritocracy is the organizing principle (if not often the reality) behind all of the stories in these pages, including my own. One succeeds in life through one's own talent and hard work. Once upon a time, meritocracy was supposed to be progressive. The concept was used originally to contrast with inherited wealth or power—instead of success coming more or less easily because of your connections, your skin color, or your parentage, it would be based solely on your own merits. Seems fair, right? But there are two problems with this: First, modern-day meritocrats still mysteriously tend to come from the upper classes because they have greater opportunity to develop their gifts—and much greater opportunity to monetize them. (This is not to say that nobody breaks through poverty or racism. But luck, in the form of the happenstance of one's birth, is still the greatest predictor of social and economic success.)

Second, and more relevant for our purposes here, meritocracy is nihilistic and cruel. Under the meritocracy, the light of our own worth—financial and ontological—is a bicycle-powered light bulb. We have to peddle hard, continually, for it to light up. And as soon as we stop, the light flickers out. It's a world of winners and losers; the light is either on or off. We have to generate our own value. If we're unable to peddle, well, that's just too bad. The idea that we get what we earn easily slips into "we *are* what we earn." Meritocracy denies any God-given foundation of inherent worth. There's no spiritual universal basic income. It denies the idea of holiness—that we are beloved just as we are, regardless of how much we accomplish or achieve. Yes, the meritocracy gives lip service to the idea that we each have worth, but in practice, some of us are clearly worth more than others.

I have played the meritocracy game for much of my life. I worked hard in school and got good grades and good SAT scores. I was strategic about my extracurricular activities. I knew that going to a top college was beyond important; it was essential. It was dangerous not to. Without an elite college education, I would wind up among the failures of society. My light would turn off.

My peers and I all knew that we had had to find careers that we were passionate about, contributed to society, and made a lot of money. We needed to aggressively make space for ourselves in the world. We would need to elbow our way in—because no space would be held for us. No one would wait for us. No one would light a path for us. There was no cosmic guidance, nothing we were meant to be or do. There was just the clinical equation of our own desires × our talent × our hard work.

I went to an Ivy League college. My merit light was blazing. But when I got there, I was lost. What did I want to do? What did I want to be? Without the benefit of religious myths to reflect my life, I had no tools for thinking about my gifts or purpose. I floundered around, arguably wasting an elite education taking quixotic classes. I took a class on world hunger and felt only intimidated. My classmates were already deep in the field, using technical lingo I had never heard of, and several had already worked in nongovernmental organizations in foreign countries. Never mind the actual substance of what we were learning, I was out of my league in the merit game, and I felt I would never catch up.

By most external standards, I have now caught up—I led a thriving New York City congregation for twelve years, I've written and recorded an album, I've published two books and many articles. The meritocracy has rewarded me with praise and acclaim for my work, a co-op apartment in Manhattan, and enough money that my kids can take instrument lessons and go to summer camp and begin to play the merit game themselves. But in secret, for most of my life, I, like so many of my peers, have felt perpetually on the brink of failure. I peddled the bicycle as fast as I could because if I stopped, I believed that my light would go out. I was only ever as good as my last grade, my last new song, my last sermon, my last publication, or the last comment from a delighted teacher or disgruntled congregant.

I yearned to feel beloved no matter what. I am not alone in this yearning. We all crave this from our childhood and throughout our lives. This need is a fundamental spiritual need. It's reflected in the aching longing of the Psalms and in much of liturgy and religious literature generally. Alanis Morrissette expresses it in her ostensibly secular language in her song, "That I Would Be Good." The song is a plea to know one's own innate goodness, regardless of the judgment of society—a goodness that would shine "even if I did nothing" or "even if I got the thumbs down." This lyric makes no explicit reference to God or faith, but note that the phrase "that I would be good" is an incomplete phrase. The omission highlights the thing omitted. It is clearly a prayer—a prayer "that I would be good even if I did nothing . . ." It's a heart-wrenching prayer that we can fall and be caught, fail and be loved. Even if the meritocracy rejects us, our bicycle light is still lit, because we are lit from the divine illumination within.

Sand Mandalas

At the far opposite end of the spectrum of worth measurement are those who have devoted their lives to religious practice—monks and nuns. The monastic life is not a productive life, at least in modern secular terms. And the oblates must confront what it means to exist for the sake of existence, pray for the sake of prayer, and sing for the sake of song. (Apparently the great Trappist monk Thomas Merton wrestled with this question. He was fascinated with the existentialist Albert Camus and journeyed with him intellectually and spiritually into the deepest questions of life, death, purpose, and purposelessness.) There are monastics who believe that they are doing spiritual "work" in emanating loving, healing prayers or doing penance on behalf of the world, shifting our spiritual-energetic plane through their practice. But in the race of the meritocracy, monastics don't even reach the starting line. In most traditions, they do not make any significant economic contribution, and in some they don't marry or have children. They consume very little—just what they need for their own sustenance—and own nothing.

Some monastics make a point of this nonproductivity. Tibetan monks spend hours and days making beautiful mandalas out of colored sand, painstakingly, sometimes grain by grain perfecting the image of the infinite. And when they are done, they let go and pour their masterpiece into the river. Along these same lines, I once heard a story of a monastery high up in the mountains where the monks were rumored to be fully realized beings, living lives of unencumbered joy. A traveler came to visit wanting to know their secrets. He asked, "What do you do? What are your practices? Do you meditate? Do you pray? Do you chant? Do you fast? Do you work?" The monks laughed and replied, "Oh, no. We don't do any of that any more. We just sit here and let God love us." Imagine having such a profound sense of your own inherent worth that you would not have to do anything at all. Just sitting there, you would be a delight to the Divine.

Not all of us are temperamentally suited to the monastic life, and I'm not suggesting that mass monasticism would be good for humanity even if we were. But I do think we might take a page from the monastic book and live more simply to cultivate a sense of enoughness in our children and ourselves. We might take up spiritual practices in the tradition of our heritage that help us feel the cosmic delight in our very being. And if this results in decreased productivity because we are less frantic to earn our keep, so be it. Human productivity is generally no gift to planet earth. All our fellow creatures benefit when humans do less. Because of this, some environmentalists, myself included, advocate for "de-growth"—an intentional shrinking of the economy. I might also call it "regrowth." We regrow in a different direction. Our souls expand when we know that we are loved, and we have less need for material success or the approval of others.

Organic Time versus Commodity Time

In the writings of Rabbi Zalman Shachter-Shalomi, the founder of the Jewish Renewal movement, he lays out the concept of "organic time" versus "commodity time." Organic time, as it sounds, is time that flows naturally, without intervention. This is the quality of time during Shabbat/Sabbath. It's the time it takes for the next wave to crash on the shore, the time it takes for a molecule of air to end up on the other side of the world, the time it takes for an embryo to become a fetus and then a baby and then to be born; there is a time for a baby to nurse and then a time to naturally wean from nursing. It's the time it takes for the sun to rise and set and rise again, from one Sabbath to the next. In nature, many things happen very, very slowly and unevenly. We use the term "glacial" to mean almost ludicrously slow—the pace of the movement of a glacier. "There is a season for every activity under the heavens," writes the Ecclesiastes author. Humans are born into organic time.

Commodity time, on the other hand, is the socially constructed flow of time. It is fast and regimented, driven by the clock and by human deadlines. Concepts of multitasking and efficiency and "time is money" fit within this framework. From the perspective of commodity time, we have such limited lifespans, time is our most precious resource. We had best make the most of it and not waste a second.

Commodity time is the prevailing understanding of time in our culture. We are constantly trying to get more done, carving up our calendars into smaller and smaller increments, scheduling our children's lives, and hiring time management specialists to help us do this better and better. Referring to factory efficiency, Karl Marx called it "closing the pores of time." Our calendar day starts at midnight—an arbitrary moment in the night—instead of at sunrise or sunset. Natural cycles, instead of seeming beautifully cyclical, seem pointlessly circular. As adults many of us start to feel uncomfortable with time that we can't control. We try to intervene in organic time, to reel it in and render it predictable and profitable.

Understandably, we feel the pressure of a ticking clock because we don't live forever. We want to squeeze as much living out of life as possible. But this pace of life doesn't come naturally to us. It can be soul crushing. It's certainly not the pace that we experienced when we were infants. When we were infants, we could spend half an hour staring at the blades of a ceiling fan going round and round. Was this a waste of time? Should we have, instead, been trying to learn to count our toes or spell our names?

Throughout my pregnancy and maternity leave, one song ran through my head almost continuously: John Lennon's "Watching the Wheels," written by Lennon after he and Yoko Ono had "dropped out" of public life. He was enjoying his days as a stay-at-home dad and described his experience as, "I'm just sittin' here watching the wheels go round and round. I really love to watch them roll. . . ." This was an organic experience of time, and far from being just a personal indulgence, Lennon believed that cultivating this kind of "drop out" consciousness would bring peace to the world. It was a radical rebuttal to the ethic of capitalism in that it prioritized relationships, family, children, and spiritual wholeness.

Hearing this story, one might object to the notion that there was anything "radical" here; it was only because of Lennon's great wealth that he was able to make this choice to stop working and care for his child full time. And this is absolutely true. What kind of society have we built where most parents cannot afford to be expansively present with their children during their precious early years (and where most who could afford to choose careerism instead)? And what does it do to children to be raised in such a society, always rushed and systematically separated from their families?

The Deathbed Test

This fault line between organic and commodity time is ever present in our society. We gear our psychic metabolism toward one side or the other—some of us seek to submit to the rhythms of nature, others seek to optimize our time and productivity. The tension takes particularly intense form in two opposing philosophical camps on childbirth and childrearing.

On one side, you have the advocates of home births, unmedicated and unmediated by doctors. In this system, babies "choose their own birthday" and labor is never induced or rushed. Everything is allowed to happen on the baby's terms. True die-hards of this philosophy even advocate for what is known as a "lotus birth," in which even violence against the umbilical cord is eschewed—the cord is not cut at all, but rather the placenta is delivered and then just placed next to the baby on a diaper for several days until it dries up and falls off on its own timetable. Proponents of natural childbirth say that the body, left to its own schedule, knows how to deliver a baby and that a baby knows how to be born. They say that the interventionist and over-medicalized births of today rob women of their innate wisdom and power and often do spiritual violence to babies.

In the other camp, there are those who say that "the natural" is overrated. They point out that until recent medical advances came along, childbirth was the leading killer of women, and the infant mortality rate was much higher than it is today. They believe that hospital births are a godsend and that mothers and babies are now healthier and happier than ever. They say that there is a right time for babies to be born and that once you get past that date the baby is fully baked and it's best to just get it out. Once labor has begun, many hospitals will establish a timeline—the labor must progress toward delivery at a certain rate or else drugs will be administered to speed things along. One in five births are medically induced in this country. And then once born, we are forever telling our children to hurry up.

For people to remain enmeshed in commodity time when they become parents benefits the economy as a whole and the corporations that drive it. Starting with medicalized birth, purchased formula, cribs, tricked-out strollers, and all the must-have baby paraphernalia, then a quick return to work with a solid night's sleep and paid childcare—it all amounts to billions and billions of dollars spent by parents and earned by corporations. Most of this commerce would be circumvented if at least one parent were able to remain in organic time with their young children. Again, this is not a critique of individuals who follow this path, but of the larger systems that leave us little real choice. It's profit extracted at the expense of families.

As you might guess, when it comes to childbirth and childcare, I fall much closer to the natural childbirth and attachment parenting side of things, and I had the privilege of being somewhat able to take the first year slower. But when my twins were infants, I found myself impatient sometimes with the glacial pace of the day. I would be tempted to multitask while nursing, to talk on the phone or read the news. On a typical morning, one of my children, my son in particular, would be nursing, and he would fall asleep against my chest. But if I tried to lay him down for a nap, he would wake up immediately and protest. Apparently, he wasn't done with his meal yet. So he'd nurse a while longer and then fall asleep again. Part of me wanted to say to him, "Look. Either eat or sleep! Just make up your mind so I can get on with my day."

But my son was my teacher in those moments. He reminded me of what I know in my heart to be true: that there is, in fact, no better use of my time. There is no better use of my time than allowing my children to live their natural rhythms. There is no better use of my time than feeling my son or daughter's warm body against me, their gentle breath rising and falling, nestled and dreaming in perfect safety and comfort. Perhaps, instead of trying to teach them the efficiencies of the adult world, I could relearn from them how to surrender to the moment.

When I question whether I should indulge my children or myself in this way, I subject the question to what I call the "deathbed test." When I am lying on my deathbed, will I wish that I had done it differently? Will I regret not having gotten more done today? Will I wish that I had pried my children off and washed the dishes or checked my email? I'm pretty sure I won't. If anything, I will wish that I had slowed down even more and savored these moments even more fully.

I think if we all gave ourselves the "deathbed test," we would come to similar conclusions. In fact, it's the things that happen at glacial pace that are often the most meaningful and lasting: the pace of real change, the pace of an infant working their way through a meal, the pace of a blade of grass growing in the spring, the pace of prayer. This is the natural pace of the *nefesh* and the pace of the *adamah*.

When we are lying on our deathbeds, if we have the luxury of reviewing our lives, I believe that we'll wish we had spent more time just sitting with the people we loved. We'll wish we had spent more time lying in a field at night, looking up at the starry sky; more time walking a city block with our children, answering every question and examining each crack in the sidewalk with them; more time enjoying every spoonful of a hot soup on a rainy afternoon; more time listening to our favorite pieces of music over and over again; more time listening to our partners and holding them after they had a hard day; more time staring at a ceiling fan, watching it go round and round.

As it turned out, John Lennon did not have all the time in the world. He died too suddenly and too young and without a deathbed on which to ponder his life. But the lyrics of his song still call to us all these years after his death as a testimony of how he chose to spend what turned out to be his latter days. He was ultimately converted from a human *doing* in commodity time to a human *being* in organic time. He spent his last days just watching the wheels go round and round, and we can guess that he died a happy man. We should all be so lucky.

Worrying Just
the Right Amount

If we want to live a religious life, or simply a life of greater vibrancy and connection to *nefesh*, *am*, and *adamah*, how much should we worry about our participation in the secular world? It depends on who we ask. In the Christian world, as in the Jewish world, there has been an ethic of adaptation to modern society—in fact, much of mainline Protestantism has become a close bedfellow to capitalism. Christian conservative Rod Dreher, in his book *The Benedict Option*, disparages this modern Christianity as merely the "chaplaincy to consumerism." He cites surveys in which 61 percent of Christian young adults had no problem at all with materialism and consumerism. Another 30 percent had some qualms but thought it was not worth worrying about. Dreher describes the United States as a post-Christian nation. His writing is saturated with the fear of cultural and spiritual annihilation.

His prescription is for Christians to beat a "strategic retreat." They should learn from the early Christians and radically separate from mainstream society, forming subcultures with their own schools, communities, and cultural institutions. He writes,

> We Christians in the West are facing our own thousand-year flood—or if you believe Pope Emeritus Benedict XVI, a fifteen-hundred year flood: in 2012, the then-pontiff said that the spiritual crisis overtaking the West is the most serious since the fall of the Roman Empire near the end of the fifth century. The light of Christianity is flickering out all over the West. There are people alive today who may live to see the effective death of Christianity within our civilization.

To some, this may seem paranoid. Liberal Christians might counter that the light of Christianity is not flickering out; it's merely changing, and in some cases growing closer to the spirit of what Jesus taught. They would claim that we have simply chosen option 3 in the 1-2-3 Crash—the option of renewing and reimagining the tradition—and are evolving with the times. And while this is certainly part of the story, such apologists also have a blind spot into which Dreher and his allies are trying to shine a spotlight.

In *The Benedict Option*, Dreher refers to the work of sociologist Christian Smith, whose research has found that among young Christians, fewer than half said that their personal moral beliefs are grounded in the Bible or any other religious sensibility. Christianity is becoming irrelevant even to Christians. Instead, young Christians and young Americans in general subscribe to moralistic therapeutic deism (MTD)—what Dreher sees as a kind of lukewarm "Christianity lite." While the values of MTD are perfectly legitimate values, Dreher points out that they have little to do with biblical or traditional Christianity, which, in his words, "teaches repentance, self-sacrificial love, and purity of heart, and commends suffering—the Way of the Cross—as the pathway to God."

The amorality of young people that Christian Smith's research found is consistent with what I found when I taught a religion class at St. Francis College in Brooklyn. The class was "Social Justice and Ecology in the Hebrew Bible," and despite this being a historically Catholic college, my students were minimally to not at all religiously engaged. More disturbingly, they were cynical. We would discuss the *mitzvot*—the commandments—of the Hebrew Bible, which, among other things, were intended to create a society that cares for the poor and the stranger and for the land itself. There would come a point in every class discussion when a student would say, "I don't know what the point of all this is; people are just going to do what they're going to do anyway." There was always a wistful sadness behind these words, as if the student longed to be convinced otherwise, but everyone would look at each other, and no one would disagree.

Beyond this defeatism, many students positively embraced materialist ideals and secular measures of success. "It's a world of winners and losers," one said, defending the ethic of competition. Another said, "If you're rich you probably deserve it, and you should spend your money however you please." These were working-class students, some immigrants, many of whom were working full-time jobs while attending college, and many who were in poor health. Their realpolitik perspective was hard earned. In our secular capitalist regime *without* a mandate to care for the poor, the stranger, or the land, and with so little support for people who are struggling, idealism has become a luxury. The idea of religion as a countercultural force was foreign.

The Slave Bible

But religious teachings have often been a countercultural force, and where powerful interests have recognized the threat that these teachings posed, they have done their best to suppress their transmission. When missionaries came to bring the gospel to the trafficked workers in the British West Indies, they brought with them a special edition of the Bible called the Slave Bible. This Bible was just like a regular Bible except that it left out 90 percent of the Hebrew Bible and 50 percent of the New Testament. It left out the stories of liberation like the exodus from Egypt; it left out the universalist teachings of Paul. It censored anything that might prompt rebellion or propagate ideas of inherent human value and belovedness. It's telling that most of the Bible was recognized as explosive material if it got into the hands of the oppressed.

Ultimately the project of keeping these ideas from the enslaved workers failed. The ideas welled up in human hearts and minds and passed from soul to soul as they have from the beginning of history. The message of the burning bush traveled across time and space. As Dr. King said in his "Letter from Birmingham Jail," writing many years later, "Oppressed people cannot remain oppressed forever. The yearning for freedom eventually manifests itself, and that is what has happened to the American Negro. Something within has reminded him of his birthright of freedom." A person can be born into slavery, but no one is born a slave.

Worrying about Assimilation

In contrast to Dreher's anxious prescription for a strategic retreat from American society, in progressive Jewish circles today, it's generally considered déclassé to worry about assimilation. The line of reassurance goes that if Judaism has survived this long in diaspora, steeped in foreign cultures, changing them and being changed by them, translating itself and adapting time and again, it must be extraordinarily resilient. And what's more, its flexibility is the key to its resiliency. Judaism changes, and Judaism thrives. The American experiment will be no exception. We also like to think that as modern, liberal Jews we are more friend than foe to our surrounding culture. Today's surrounding culture is largely secular (or religious communities that have themselves assimilated to secular capitalism). We think of the alternative—religious separatism—as regressive and suffocating.

But I suspect that when religious communities fail, their dissolution can be attributed to an overly laissez-faire attitude toward various kinds of intercourse with the wider community. What can be celebrated in one generation as rich, creative syncretism can in retrospect be revealed to be the beginning of the slippery slope of assimilation landing in a puddle of slush at the bottom of the slide.

When a small community is plunked down in a vast sea of a different culture that is compelling, powerful, not too hostile, and where money can be made, it's all too easy to find reasons to adopt their ways and let go of one's own. With each generation the thread of identity and practice, stories and spirituality grows thinner and thinner—and the identification with the dominant culture and its values grows stronger and stronger—until there is nothing left but a few wisps of old customs performed for the sake of nostalgia.

I'm not suggesting that everyone needs to be orthodox in their own tradition. But I am concerned that in progressive circles our heartfelt desire for a universalist inclusivity (and to not be embarrassingly at war with "normal" culture) may blind us to the power of secular American capitalism and to the fragility of the particular religious consciousness with which we have been entrusted. The power differential is too vast to be treated casually. If we want to reconnect to the beauty and power of our lineages, there are times we need to be fierce and draw lines and make choices or risk losing everything. Sabbath practice offers a perfect example of the line-drawing fierceness that is required.

Sabbath as Resistance and Renewal

Religious traditions offer spiritual technologies for regrounding and *teshuvah*, returning to our holy center. But while many of us will eagerly try meditation apps on our phones, coloring books, or power yoga, many of us bristle at the idea of a committed, old-fashioned religious practice like Sabbath practice. Even those of us who wish we had more time for ourselves and families and who like the idea of Sabbath time—tend to be skeptical that a bunch of rules is necessary.

A former congregant of mine, Joy, tells a story of what happened when she and her husband Joe decided that the Sabbath rules they had followed their whole lives were unnecessarily strict. As she tells it, the beginning of the end of her Sabbath practice came one Sunday when she realized they were out of cinnamon. Her Mormon faith taught that you don't go shopping on Sundays, but she needed cinnamon for the special meal she was preparing for her family. It was a key ingredient. So she discussed it with her husband, and they decided that they would go just this once and just buy the cinnamon and nothing else. They would still stay internally in the spirit of the Sabbath the whole time. So they went out and bought the cinnamon with seemingly no ill effects.

Joy has happy memories of Sabbath with her family growing up. They went to church in the morning, baked cookies in the afternoon, listened to special music, made dinner all together and then spent hours at the table, just hanging out talking and being silly and laughing. Sunday nights they would all pile onto their parents' bed and watch G-rated movies. When she left home, Joy missed those family Sundays. But as she grew older, she moved away from Mormonism—among other things she objected to LDS church's conservative stances on gay marriage and gender roles. The Sabbath rules, along with all religious rules, had come to feel less important, hence the cinnamon incident.

The next week it was cheese. "It would be so nice to have some cheese to go with dinner tonight, let's go out and just get some cheese. Nothing else." While they were at the store, they picked up some bread too. To go with the cheese. Again, no ill effects. The next Sunday, it was, "Well, while we're here at the store we might as well just zip around and do a little shopping for the week, just a quick one to get us through since we're out of a bunch of stuff." It's easy to imagine how it progressed, Sunday after Sunday. Food shopping became a regular fixture of the day, then laundry. They told each other, "We're still keeping the spirit of the Sabbath with our special meal and special Sabbath music."

Joe was fighting a deadline one Sunday and needed to do just a little work. Joy decided, "If he's working, I might as well get something done too." Now they were both working and shopping and running errands on Sundays. Their special dinners fell away, and the special music fell away. And pretty soon Sunday became, in Joy's words, "just another day." And it was right around that time when they noticed that they were experiencing their lifetime peak of Sunday night anxiety. They used to coast to the end of their Sabbath feeling rested and centered. Now they were getting things done on Sundays, but they had never felt more stressed. By Sunday night they were tired, fighting with each other, overwhelmed. For the first time in their lives, they felt like they could hardly face the week ahead.

Joy and Joe's cautionary tale makes a strong case for "rules." They assumed that a small purchase on the Sabbath would be harmless, when in fact it wound up chipping away at their spiritual practice until there was nothing left. It is said that absolute abstinence is easier than perfect moderation. Making exceptions and partial commitments to a practice can actually be much harder than staying in with both feet. The slide of secularism is slippery. Had Joy and Joe been able to continue to observe the seemingly arbitrary Mormon Sabbath rules, they might have preserved something that was precious to them both.

To keep religious practices like Sabbath in our world—to resist the highly sophisticated seduction techniques of consumer capitalism in which teams of PhD psychologists are constantly working to perfectly trigger our deepest, most primal longings 24/7—requires the fierceness of a warrior. It requires a willingness to forcefully reject what is deemed normal and harmless in our world and see it for what it is. It requires a countercultural fire rising up from the ancient coals of our religious lineage. To truly mount a *teshuvah*—a return to our own bodies, community, and the earth—we must be willing to live in such a way that we may be seen as freaks by our peers—until they can be persuaded to join us.

Technological Determinism

This kind of assertion of a religious practice over and against our modern cultural norms is quite foreign to most of us, especially on the left, and especially when those norms have to do with technology. People will say that it's simply not "realistic." What strikes me most painfully as I talk with people about the screen-based life we now lead is the sense of utter resignation to it. Very much like COVID-19 itself, people now believe that internet technology is a permanent feature of our lives; the best we can do is limit our exposure and try to not let it harm us too much or kill us too often. Even those who believe that it's unhealthy for themselves or their children to spend hours in front of screens speak of addressing it only in terms of moderation and titration.

Outside of some Amish, Mennonite, and ultra-orthodox Jewish communities that avoid the internet, I don't know of a single person who practices vigorous resistance, not to mention complete abstinence. I'm sure such people exist, but I would not know them because they have placed themselves outside of the circles of mainstream society. By keeping their *nefesh* intact and interacting with others only in person, they have made themselves culturally invisible. This is how deeply online existence has been woven into our consciousness in less than a generation.

Ours has become an increasingly depressed society, all the more so as the virtual way of life has crept into every crevice of our culture. Every day it seems new studies come out that carefully, gingerly, with many caveats, show a link between our screens and our collective silent scream. Growing evidence connects social media use with social anxiety, eating disorders, and even higher suicide rates, especially among teenagers. But we collectively shrug. What can be done? We have been trained to look for comfort to the very source of our despair. Like a mosquito, it injects a numbing agent before it sucks our blood.

Try to place any real restrictions on your children's technology use, keep them off of social media, or, God forbid, not give them a smartphone to begin with, and other parents will laugh at you. They will shake their heads and say with the authority of experience, "You will lose." I've noticed that people get a little defensive at the suggestion that our tech use is optional. When I mention that I avoid shopping on Amazon—usually in response to a cheerful "you can get it on Amazon for only $7.69"—I often get a slightly sarcastic response: "Well, that must be nice." "Lucky you that you have so much free time." Sometimes, if the friend is appalled as I am by Amazon's depredations, the response can be more wistful: "I wish I could do that." But among most of my peers, and I suspect among most people in the United States, to want to avoid Amazon is snobbery; to be able to avoid it is privilege.

You, the reader, may be nodding your head with this. You too believe that there's no going back. You can't roll back the clock. It's so self-evidently true, it's not even worth discussing. But I have come to believe that this philosophy of technological determinism, where we are inevitably, progressively, and inescapably dragged into a techno-future, is itself the army inside the Trojan horse. It is a prime strategy of learned helplessness, to keep us from resisting. Why resist something that's inevitable? It's naive. It's laughable.

Journalist Ezra Klein observes how we insulate technology from criticism:

American culture remains deeply uncomfortable with technological critique. There is something akin to an immune system against it: You get called a Luddite, an alarmist. "In this sense, all Americans are Marxists," [Neil] Postman wrote, "for we believe nothing if not that history is moving us toward some preordained paradise and that technology is the force behind that movement."

I think that's true, but it coexists with an opposite truth: Americans are capitalists, and we believe nothing if not that if a choice is freely made, that grants it a presumption against critique. That is one reason it's so hard to talk about how we are changed by the mediums we use. That conversation, on some level, demands value judgments.

Once again, our revulsion at old-school religious fire-and-brimstone judgment makes us allergic to any form of judgment at all, particularly when the thing to be judged was freely chosen by "the people." The people's freedom is unquestionable. ("The most important thing is to never make them feel guilty.") When there is no God, as Cicero put it, "Vox populi, vox Dei" (the voice of the people is the voice of God). Accordingly, adaptation to cultural norms—rather than resistance—is a virtue. In fact, in another instance of Unitarian Universalism making explicit the implicit theologies of modernity, a new statement of faith adopted by the Unitarian Universalist Association in 2024 affirms a central shared value of nonresistance: "Transformation—We adapt to a changing world."

Karl Marx famously wrote the following about the role of religion in the people's subjugation to capitalism:

> Religion is the sigh of the oppressed creature, the heart of a heartless world, just as it is the spirit of a spiritless situation. It is the opium of the people. The abolition of religion as the illusory happiness of the people is required for their real happiness.

> The demand to give up the illusion about its condition is the demand to give up a condition which needs illusions.

The religious forms of Marx's time and place probably did keep the people demure and obedient. But if Marx were alive today, I feel certain that he would see our internet-based technologies as performing the same function. It is now technology that is the co-optive, gaslighting friend of capitalism, and it is religious community that is a potential outpost of resistance. Replace each instance of the word "religion" with "internet technology" in the quote above, and it rings true. Marx might note that as consumer religion has receded from public life in Western nations, the forces of capitalism searched for a successor. They found it online.

Especially with the assistance of religious firepower, I do not believe that any aspect of our socially constructed world is inevitable or unchangeable. I believe that we are endowed with the capacity to transform. But neither is it inevitable that we will change. If we want this world to be different, we will have to all put the work in and be prepared for some discomfort as we challenge fundamental social norms.

I imagine that in this work, we might try to conjure the energy of the "wrathful deities" of Tibetan Buddhism. These are the deities dedicated to destroying spiritual adversaries—the obstacles to meditation and personal liberation. These deities are traditionally depicted with necklaces made of the skulls of their enemies, oven with a foot on the prone body of a victim. They ultimately do their gory work for the sake of compassion. But they are fierce, and unleashing their energy can be dangerous. This is the power that we need to bring to the battle to reclaim our birthright as embodied humans grounded in earth and community.

Days of Awe

When I told a friend the title of this book, *The Secret Despair of the Secular Left*, she responded immediately with a wry smile, "Is it really so secret?" Unexpectedly, my heart sang. No, it's not so secret. It's not secret at all. The despair, the grief, and the unrealized loss—deep down in our soul-bodies many of us are experiencing these things, and we know it. We may not often admit it in polite company, and we may not always connect the dots between our malaise and our modern secular lifeways, but our hearts yearn for more.

We are exhausted from the effort of our *nefesh* rushing back and forth between our bodies and the virtual world. We are lonely from the disintegration of the *am*—the warm community of our people. And we are disoriented by our estrangement from *adamah*, our earth mother. Everything feels a bit sterile. We were made for a life of greater joy and fecundity, of beating hearts and surging libidos. We know it. It's no secret. And our souls are frustrated—separated from this life by the thin condom of our culture. It's almost invisible and yet felt by so many of us.

In writing this book, I have often wondered why the writing has felt so good. On its face, it does not seem like it should be a cheery enterprise. But I came to understand that in naming the grief and recognizing these losses of our time, I was bearing witness to that which risks being lost in myself—the tender, wild essence of my own *nefesh*. Each story of grief shared by a friend or congregant resonated deeply with me as if I were listening to my own child-self crying out for nourishment. To commit it all to writing is to offer that child a compassionate witness: "I hear you. I believe you. And, no, it shouldn't be this way." The relief of recognition is palpable.

Teshuvah

The concept of *teshuvah* is, to me, one of the most powerful concepts in Judaism. Often translated as "repentance," it more accurately means "return," as in a return to God or a return to the sacred self. *Teshuvah* boldly affirms that there *is* a sacred self. There is a primal wholeness to which we can return from our fragmentation, individually and collectively. It is not something to be added on—it is foundational. It's already here, in us, in this world, now. Wholeness still exists, in both memory and potential, ready to be realized by our process of *teshuvah*.

The medieval Jewish philosopher Maimonides laid out a detailed process of *teshuvah* in his classic work *Mishneh Torah*. This process is crisply outlined in a recent book by Rabbi Danya Ruttenberg in the form of five steps: (1) Naming and owning harm—admitting specifically what we did and articulating why it was harmful. (2) Starting an internal change—beginning the work of understanding why we did what we did so that we'll be able to make different choices. (3) Restitution and accepting consequences—doing whatever we can to heal what was harmed or finding a way to make a positive contribution. (4) Apology—apologizing to those we harmed in a way that centers their needs. (5) Making different choices—when faced with a similar situation in the future, we act differently and don't repeat our actions from the past.

Although these were intended as a roadmap for a sinner in the Middle Ages, they also strike me as tailormade for our modern collective sin predicament—for all of us who are both victims and perpetrators of our alienation from the divine. It's a practical and wise approach to a global-scale problem. Because if someone were to tell us, "Just stop living the entire way you're living and do everything differently," we would laugh at them. Even if they were to tell us to pick one thing—"Just move back to your hometown," or "Just get married"—that could also be extremely difficult given the centrifugal pressures we face. There's a lot from which to extricate ourselves. We can't jump straight to solutions without, as Einstein taught, first spending 55 minutes deeply understanding the problem, and, I would add, allowing ourselves to really feel the grief.

Four of the five of Maimonides's steps of *teshuvah* are about just that. They are forms of reckoning with where we are right now, what our lives are really like, what we've lost, what we've taken from others, and why we feel despair. This is a process in which any of us can engage. It's not only a prerequisite, but an essential component of making change. And, if my experience is any indication, it can be deeply satisfying work—because it asks us to hold a microphone to that muted voice crying out from our souls and from the earth. It feels good to recognize that voice. It is not a process of blame or guilt, but of cherishing our tender selves and making a promise of return. An honest reckoning is sweet medicine for the helplessness that many of us feel these days.

I am reminded here again of the beautiful *teshuvah* of some of the Indigenous peoples of North America as recounted by Carol Lee Sanchez. As she tells it, there was a time when the community had engaged in "such wasteful and destructive hunting practices that many species of animals were reduced to endangered levels." What's most remarkable, she points out, is that later generations did not try to cover up this painful story. "On the contrary," she writes, "the stories of those events which caused so much suffering ... are solemnly recited at various times during the year. This is done so the members of those Tribes would always remember what happened ... and thus never bring about such destructive conditions again." It became part of the oral history.

Sanchez also recounts that the turning point came when the tribes remembered how to ask the elements of the earth for help in changing the way they were living. She writes, "As a group, they asked to be forgiven. As a group, they asked for guidance. As a group they sought to re-establish their connection to all the things in their environment." She says that once they did this, they received the guidance they had prayed for. They followed the guidance and began to make change. Soon the streams were flowing abundantly again and the animals and medicine plants surged back. This whole process of return echoes Maimonides's steps of *teshuvah*. They named and acknowledged the harm done and took steps of internal change so they could do it differently in the future. They asked for forgiveness and began the work of restitution. The people returned to the earth, and the life force returned abundantly to the people.

Without claiming parity of my efforts with the grandeur of this story, I'd like to believe that writing this book has been a beginning of a process of *teshuvah* for our time. I have tried to name and articulate specifically how our secular libertine lifeways have been draining our life force. I have begun the work of internal change by seeking to understand why we participate in these systems and what brought us to this point. I've tried to take part in healing through listening and affirmation as people told me their stories of grief. And I have beamed apology to my own child-self for the ways I have muted her song in this often tone-deaf world.

Maimonides's final step of *teshuvah* contains yet another powerful principle: he says that we know that our process of *teshuvah* is complete when the situation in which we sinned comes up again, and this time we make a different choice. This raises the inevitable question, "What if a similar situation never comes up again?" Rabbi Alan Lew, who has written extensively on this topic, says, "Don't worry; it will!" Because the actions we take that are out of alignment with our higher self or the health of our ecosystems are not random. They are symptoms of something in us that needs attention, and something in our society that needs attention.

Everything we experience on the personal level is a fractal mirror of something on the collective level, and vice versa. The places of constriction within us form patterns that play out again and again in the world. And our actions ripple outward and touch everything: the *adamah* herself is exquisitely responsive to each of her parts. This is why the work of *teshuvah*, when done right, is deep inner work and deep outer work. The more we delve into it, the deeper it goes. It can open up into a huge psychic cavern.

God willing, if we live long enough, we will have a chance to face our collective demons many times. We will have many opportunities to move toward transformation, many turns up at bat. In Jewish tradition there is a focused season for *teshuvah*—the time leading up to Rosh Hashanah (the New Year) through Yom Kippur (the Day of Atonement). This is a luminous time of year when we endeavor to stage a great return. Of course we should engage in *teshuvah* every day, but it is believed that at this time of year we have a special spiritual wind at our back. We have extra change-making powers. It is a time when the veil between us and the divine is thin—we can feel the electricity in the air and wonder at the miraculous human capacity to transform. These days in between Rosh Hashanah and Yom Kippur are aptly known as the Days of Awe.

Awe

I'm coming home from dropping my kid off at school on a beautiful spring day, and I see that some city workers are trimming a tree and there are branches scattered on the ground. It just so happens that the tree is in bloom at the time, and so I scoop up a few of these flowering branches and bring them home with me. (Anyone who has ever dated me, and the one now married to me, has early on come to the distressing realization that I actually dislike receiving beautiful flowers that are chopped down in their prime and given to me as a symbol of love, only to watch them slowly die on the kitchen table.) But these flowers are free. They are otherwise destined for the woodchipper. So I am thrilled to be able to bring them home and put them in water and admire their beauty.

From high up in the tree, these branches look like they're just covered with a pale, soft glow. Looking at them more closely when I get them home, I realize that the glow is actually made up of individual tufts, each about the size of a fist. And each tuft is really a cluster of individual flowers. Each flower is comprised of tiny petals, each about the size of a pinky fingernail. I start counting: 5 petals per flower, 20 flowers per cluster. That's 100 petals per cluster. How many clusters of flowers are there on those couple branches I brought home? About twenty. 20 × 100? 2,000. There were 2,000 petals gracing these branches now on my kitchen table—just trimmings from an ordinary, medium-sized tree. 2,000 petals. I think I hear God chuckle at my amazement.

> ME: "That's impossible. How could there be that many? I must have done the math wrong."
> GOD: "Count 'em yourself if you really must quantify these things. Actually, don't. I'll just tell you. It's 2,439."
> ME: "Okay. . . ."
> GOD: "That's nothing. *Nothing*. When you're going outside sometime, let me know. I'll go with you and you'll see."

So a few days later, I'm out running and I go to the Ramble in Central Park. The Ramble is a forested section of the park with a lake in the middle of it, and I am fortunate to live within running distance. I find a corner of the lake where there aren't many people, and I look around. Flowering trees are everywhere in spectacular bloom. I think about the branches at home with over 2,000 petals on them. Each of these trees, bursting with branches just like that. This tree right in front of me: hundreds of thousands, maybe even millions of petals on it. "That's 2,438,355," says God. I hear the laughter again.

There are birds, too, all around me—reds, grays, browns, making a holy racket. I'm dizzied by the effortless abundance of it all; each tree swaying in the breeze, each bush, each bird just a gesture, an easy splash of color. Looking at the kaleidoscope all around me, the explosions of life in every direction, the delicious volatility, the vibrations of sound, the unfathomable scale—there are no words, there are no numbers to express this extravagance.

The lake is another dash of divine humor. "You want it all doubled?" says God, "Poof!" It's all there again in mirror image on the surface of the water. "You want it tripled? You want it quadrupled? I spin off whole universes before you've had breakfast." The giddy playfulness of creation; the humor. I feel joy welling up in me. Awe. I feel profound awe.

Awe is a spiritual word, and indeed a religious word that fills the liturgical literature in many traditions. It suggests something bigger even than amazement. I think of it as the dawning awareness of the presence of the Divine—something greater, something beyond ourselves, beyond our control and beyond our comprehension. It can feel thrilling, humbling, terrifying, liberating, even comforting. Awe is soul nourishment. In the experience of awe, there can be no boredom. Life feels vibrant and purposeful, like we are part of a grand cosmic project yearning toward wholeness. It puts us each in our place as one petal—one beautiful, fragrant, essential petal—out of billions. The more we know and the more we open ourselves to it, the more it can fill our consciousness. Awe is an antidote to the despair of our time.

Einstein famously said, "There are two ways to live life: one is as if nothing is a miracle and the other is as if everything is a miracle." What a difference this shift in perspective makes. If nothing is a miracle, our stance toward the natural world is one of extraction and control. If everything is a miracle, it is one of awe and reverence. If nothing is a miracle, the material world and all the people in it are just resources to be shaped and used. If everything is a miracle, each creature is infused with the holy and each *nefesh* is of infinite value. If nothing is a miracle, we languish. If everything is a miracle, we blossom.

I believe that the culture of "nothing is a miracle" is the secular culture of anxiety and depression, screens and consumer toys, and it's the extractive culture that is driving our ecosystems to the edge of collapse. To begin to heal our relationship with each other and with the rest of creation, we need to transform that culture. We need a collective *teshuvah* of return to awe.

Spiritual and culture change is slow but powerful. It's like planting the seed of a flowering tree. Whether we experience a personal God who has snarky conversations with us and calculates the number of petals on a tree, or we use religious technologies to connect to the ineffable grandeur of the universe, we can each find our own pathways to awe. We can make time for it in our week and in our day. Prayer, meditation, music, blessings before meals. Practicing together in religious community. Asking for guidance. Giving ourselves the open space to notice how miraculous everything really is. Because it really is, beginning with the fact that there is something rather than nothing.

Our souls on their cosmic journey have manifested as bodies in this physical world just briefly. We each get a window of consciousness in this life, like the shutter of a camera opening and closing in an instant. This is our big opportunity for embodiment here in the material plane. This is it. We get to experience all the sensuality of this volatile, omni-fragrant, cacophonous, everything-bagel world for just a moment. We get just one chance to love in the human ways of love.

Awe is a natural spiritual response to being alive on this earth, and it is the natural state of a small child. Yet for all the reasons I've shared in these pages, it's hard for any of us, myself included, to access our natural, wonder-filled child selves directly these days. But sometimes, if we make space for them, we can hear them quietly humming a tune or maybe cracking a joke. We can feel them longing to luxuriate in organic time, play in the dirt, and draw creativity from the well of divine inspiration. We can tap into their simple desire to be loved exactly as they are. Sometimes we can only see their outline in the negative spaces of their absence. Lifting and examining each ideological puzzle piece of our society can give a glimpse of the glowing, innocent souls that lie beneath. I pray that this glimpse can serve as the north star of our return—the journey back to our sacred body, community, and land.

In my more faith-filled moments, I can see a vision of the future, in generations to come, when we will have made that journey. We will live in a state of spiritual–earthly abundance. And we will look back on this time, today, as an aberration—a soul-diseased era when the vital signs of our collective *nefesh* were failing and the *adamah* almost vomited us out. We will not hide this from each other, but following the *teshuvah* practice of the Indigenous peoples, we will gather in our tribes and tell the stories every year. We will tell and re-tell the tales of despair and grief, how it happened, and why. And we'll teach our children how we found our way back—how we asked for divine guidance, reclaimed our sacred traditions, and regrounded. We'll tell of how we made amends and asked forgiveness not only of our neighbors and fellow creatures but of our own child-selves who had been for so long yearning for release.

We will tell of the fierceness with which we had to battle a culture that seemed so normal; how we had to resist our role as lonely, passive consumers; how we rejected the products that made our lives easier but emptier. We'll tell of how we began once again to welcome the wildness at the edges of our fields. And we'll tell of how, slowly at first, and then all at once, the change happened. We began to look each other in the eyes. We began to take each other's hands. One by one, and then all together, we began to close our computers, shut down our phones, and step outside. And when we did, we found a wonder of a world out there. It was as if a virtual veil had been lifted and we could now experience reality. Life became vivid again, and our libidos stirred. The feeling of connection was thrilling. We felt real joy for the first time in ages. This was a world worth fighting for. And from that day forward, we'll tell our children, all our days became days of awe.

Acknowledgments

"You don't write a book because you have *time* to write a book." These were the wise words of Rabbi Marcia Prager, dean emerita of the Aleph Ordination Program, where I am a rabbinical student. I had asked for her advice as to whether I should take a year off from my studies in order to write this book. Otherwise, I thought, I would never "have time." I already had a very full-time job as a parish minister, not to mention that other full-time job of mothering two tweens. But Reb Marcia's words had the clear ring of truth to them, and it thrilled me to think what it would be like to believe them. What if time really is just a construct? I already knew that in an hour I can get a lot done or get nothing done; it all depends on the quality of energy I'm able to bring to my work. And so I took the leap of faith, kept my career and my studies going, kept my kids alive, and wrote this book. I am immensely grateful to Reb Marcia for her simple but profound insight and the freedom it gave me.

Reb Marcia's message, of course, also begs the question, If not because one has time, why *does* one write a book? In my case, I wrote it because all those people and projects that were filling my life were conduits for spiritual powers, inspiring me, loving me, supporting me, challenging me, and kicking my ass until it was written.

Acknowledgments

I wrote this book because my brilliant editor, Adrienne Ingram, ignored all my various protestations (including that I didn't have time) and insisted that I submit a proposal. She believed in me—that the amorphous, discombobulated, and very private swirlings in my head could be verbalized in a way that other people could receive. And she guided me through the process with a steady hand. As I fretted about structure and scope creep, and whether I was making any sense, she repeated her mantra: "Just write." And then she helped me see what belonged, what didn't, and what more there could be. Lisa Kloskin, Erin Gibbons, and Marissa Wold Uhrina, also Broadleaf editors, as well as graphic designers Jay Smith and Kristi Smith and publicist Chloe Wertz, saw the project through to completion with kindness, patience, and exquisite attention to detail.

I wrote this book because of the loving guidance of my spiritual teachers and intellectual mentors: Rabbi Natan Margalit, Rabbi David Ingber, Rabbi Elliot Ginsberg, Rabbi Nadya Gross, Rabbi (and cousin) Jeff Marx, Dara Blumenthal, Steph Stern, and Sami Badawy. These teachers, along with those whose words I've only gotten to read in books, helped me understand today's vast social and technological currents in light of ancient mystical wisdom and of my own spiritual journey.

I wrote this book because of the gifts that my congregants gave me during my years as a UU minister in Chicago and New York, sharing their stories with me, their tender dreams, losses, hopes, and their spiritual longings that were often so similar to my own. I will be forever grateful for the time we spent together.

I wrote this book because of the hours of delicious conversations with friends who nourished my mind and stirred up my soul: Barukh Solomon, Erica Ariel Fox, Igal Harmelin, Dianne Cohler-Esses, Jen Goldman-Wetzler, and Shira Nayman, who was the first to read my complete draft and whose insights helped me immeasurably in reimagining the final chapter (and in actually understanding the book I had just written).

I wrote this book because my husband, Jeff, who more than anyone had a direct stake in my lack of "time," was relentlessly encouraging and supportive, always insisting that I prioritize my writing, picking up slack for me at home, and forever scouting for material for me ("Sweetie, I came across this thing that might be perfect for your book!"). Our long, lazy Shabbat talks were a steady stream of inspiration. Jeff's love is the nurturing earth in which I am grounded and brings forth all good fruits in my life.

And I wrote this book because my children, Miri and Micah, show me every day what's at stake in all these abstract questions of connection and disconnection. I've watched them navigate our alienated, tech-infused world, and I've seen how they are never happier than when they are exploring a forest or beach, laughing with friends, dancing, or making music. I have wanted urgently to protect sacred space and time for them to be themselves. They teach me over and over again that the path to God is through our bodies, in community with loved ones, and playing in the dirt. If this book can help open that pathway even a little bit for my children, and for all children, that will have been reason enough to write it.

Notes

Unrealized Loss

10 *"resolve a problem":* Christian Smith, *Soul Searching: The Religious and Spiritual Lives of American Teenagers* (Oxford University Press, 2009), 162–163.

15 *as they did pre-pandemic:* Emma Goldberg, "The ZIP Code Shift: Why Many Americans No Longer Live Where They Work," *New York Times*, March 4, 2024. https://www.nytimes.com/2024/03/04/business/zip-code-shift-home-work.html

17 *"'check engine' light of culture":* Thomas Hübl, *Healing Collective Trauma: A Process for Integrating Our Intergenerational and Cultural Wounds* (Sounds True, 2023), xxiv–xxv.

17 *happier than liberals:* Ross Pomeroy, "Why Are Conservatives Happier Than Liberals?" *Real Clear Science*, August 27, 2022. https://www.realclearscience.com/blog/2022/08/27/why_are_conservatives_happier_than_liberals_849615.html

The Secular Gaze

35 *"deep meditative consciousness":* Donaugh Coleman, "Presence in Death," *Spiral* (The Rubin Museum of Art, 2023).

47 *"lead to failure":* Talal Asad, *Genealogies of Religion: Discipline and Reasons of Power in Christianity and Islam* (Johns Hopkins University Press, 1993), 28.

Where Did All the Religious Flower Children Go?

51 *"'1-2-3 Crash' model":* Benay Lappe, "1, 2, 3, CRASH! How to Navigate Inevitable Change," TEDxSpenceSchool. https://www.youtube.com/watch?v=WTdeIFK7VSc

57 *"traditionalism on life support":* Shaul Magid, *American Post-Judaism: Identity and Renewal in a Post-Ethnic Society* (Indiana University Press, 2013), 112.

60 *"just not negotiable":* Lappe, "1, 2, 3, CRASH! How to Navigate Inevitable Change," TEDxSpenceSchool. https://www.youtube.com/watch?v=WTdeIFK7VSc

Loss of Intimacy

62 *"you are the product":* Jeff Orlowski, dir., *The Social Dilemma*, 2020, Netflix.

Contactless

78 *The Shock Doctrine:* Naomi Klein, *The Shock Doctrine: The Rise of Disaster Capitalism* (Picador, 2008).

88 *"turned up in Croatia":* Greg Milner, "Ignore the GPS. That Ocean Is Not a Road." *New York Times*, February 11, 2016. https://www.nytimes.com/2016/02/14/opinion/sunday/ignore-the-gps-that-ocean-is-not-a-road.html?searchResultPosition=8

92 *"brick-and-mortar retail fiasco":* Wolf Richer. "The Bloodletting Among Retailers Simply Doesn't Let Up." *Wolf Street*, March 5, 2017. https://wolfstreet.com/2017/03/05/brick-mortar-retailers-bankruptcies-restructuring-neiman-marcus-bcbg-hhgregg/

Living in a Material World

97 *"had to do with the body":* Daniel Boyarin, *Carnal Israel: Reading Sex in Talmudic Culture* (University of California Press, 1995), 1.

103 *"your life's inspiration":* Báyò Akómoláfé, interview on *The Emerald* [podcast] with Joshua Michael Schrei. April 7, 2023.

105 *"time, tradition, and culture":* Swami Satyananda Saraswati, *Kundalini* Tantra (Bihar School of Yoga, 1984), 3–4.

Pe'ah—The Wild, Holy Edge

114 *"they become black"*: Isabel Wilkerson, *Caste: The Origins of Our Discontents* (Random House Trade Paperbacks, 2023), 53.

116 *"easily acquired"*: Evan Eisenberg, *The Ecology of Eden: An Inquiry into the Dream of Paradise and a New Vision of Our Role in Nature* (Vintage Books, Random House 1998), 47.

117 *"a landscape (or several)"*: Eisenberg, *The Ecology of Eden*, 45.

119 *"unless one should see them"*: "Columbus Reports on His First Voyage, 1493." The Gilder Lehrman Institute of American History, 2010. https://www.gilderlehrman.org/sites/default/files/inline-pdfs/01427_fps.pdf

119 *Mother Earth and Father Sky:* Carol Lee Sanchez, "Animal, Vegetable, and Mineral," in *Ecofeminism and the Sacred*, edited by Carol J. Adams (Continuum; New York), 216.

120 *"one and the same"*: Roxanne Dunbar-Ortiz, *"All the Real Indians Died Off" and 20 Other Myths About Native Americans* (Beacon Press, 2016), 128.

121 *"heat comes from the furnace"*: Aldo Leopold, *A Sand County Almanac: And Sketches Here and There* (Oxford University Press, 1949), 6.

122 *Matthew Desmond:* "In Order to Understand the Brutality of American Capitalism, You Have to Start on the Plantation," *New York Times*, August 14, 2019. https://www.nytimes.com/interactive/2019/08/14/magazine/slavery-capitalism.html

123 *"a few seasons later"*: Desmond, *Brutality of American Capitalism*.

123 *"dragged out by the roots"*: Desmond, *Brutality of American Capitalism*.

It's the Thought That Counts

129 *over 47 inches:* PRNewswire, "NPD: US TV Purchasers More Motivated by Screen Size and Picture Quality Than Ever Before," *The NPD Group*, April 26, 2022. https://www.npd.com/news/press-releases/2022/npd-us-tv-purchasers-more-motivated-by-screen-size-and-picture-quality-than-ever-before/

130 *"rhetoric without further action"*: Graeme Wood, "'Land Acknowledgments' Are Just Moral Exhibitionism," *The Atlantic*, November 28, 2021. https://www.theatlantic.com/ideas/archive/2021/11/against-land-acknowledgements-native-american/620820/

Spiritual Bypass and the Caging of the Yetzer Ha-Ra

133 *"made peace with it"*: John Welwood, "On Bypassing and Spiritual Relationship," *Science and Nonduality*, February 10, 2024. https://scienceandnonduality.com/article/on-spiritual-bypassing-and-relationship/

136 *the last twenty years:* Emily Willingham, "People Have Been Having Less Sex—Whether They're Teenagers or 40-Somethings," *Scientific American*, January 3, 2022. https://www.scientificamerican.com/article/people-have-been-having-less-sex-whether-theyre-teenagers-or-40-somethings/

139 *"not a single egg could be found"*: Babylonian Talmud, Yoma 69b.

Breasts

151 *unclean drinking water:* Susan Brink, "Why the Breastfeeding Vs. Formula Debate Is Especially Critical in Poor Countries," *Goats and Soda*, NPR/WNYC, July 13, 2018. https://www.npr.org/sections/goatsandsoda/2018/07/13/628105632/is-infant-formula-ever-a-good-option-in-poor-countries

Being Worthwhile

166 *$105 billion per year:* Lauren Hoffman, "State Abortion Bans Will Harm Women and Families' Economic Security Across the U.S.," The Center for American Progress, August 25, 2022.

167 *"life hack for ambitious women"*: Anna Louie Sussman, "Tinder Drove Me to Freeze My Eggs," *The Economist*, February 14, 2022.

168 *"I can't afford to have a baby"*: Lawrence B. Finer, "Reasons U.S. Women Have Abortions: Quantitative and Qualitative Perspectives," Perspectives on Sexual and Reproductive Health, Guttmacher Institute, vol. 37, no. 3, September 2005.

---

131 *"could only happen here"*: Sophie Lewis, "Raphael Warnock's Victory Speech Honors Mother's '82-Year-Old Hands That Used to Pick Somebody Else's Cotton,'" *CBS News*, January 6, 2021. https://www.cbsnews.com/news/raphael-warnock-victory-speech-mother-united-states-senate-election-georgia-06-01-2021/

169 ***"an act of patriotism":*** Jimmy Carter, "Crisis of Confidence," delivered July 15, 1979: https://www.pbs.org/wgbh/americanexperience/features/carter-crisis/
169 ***global greenhouse gas emissions:*** Ezra Klein, "The Hidden Cost of Cheap Meat," Ezra Klein podcast, *New York Times*, November 29, 2022. https://www.nytimes.com/2022/11/29/opinion/ezra-klein-podcast-leah-garces.html
172 ***"what it means to be fully human":*** Sohrab Ahmari, *The Unbroken Thread* (Convergent Books/Random House, 2021), 5–7.

Worrying Just the Right Amount

188 ***"Christianity within our civilization":*** Rod Dreher, *The Benedict Option: A Strategy for Christians in a Post-Christian Nation* (Sentinel/Penguin Random House, 2017), 8.
197 ***"demands value judgments":*** Ezra Klein, "I Didn't Want It to Be True, but the Medium Really Is the Message," *New York Times*, August 7, 2022. https://www.nytimes.com/2022/08/07/opinion/media-message-twitter-instagram.html
198 ***"a condition which needs illusions":*** Karl Marx, "Introduction." *A Contribution to the Critique of Hegel's Philosophy of Right*, translated by A. Jolin and J. O'Malley, edited by J. O'Malley. Cambridge University Press, [1843] 1970.

Days of Awe

200 ***five steps:*** Danya Ruttenberg, *On Repentance and Repair: Making Amends in an Unapologetic World* (Beacon Press, 2023), 26–45.
202 ***"such destructive conditions again":*** Sanchez, "Animal, Vegetable, and Mineral," 215.
202 ***medicine plants surged back:*** Sanchez, "Animal, Vegetable, and Mineral," 216.